Competing for Employees

*Proven Marketing Strategies
for Hiring and Keeping
Exceptional People*

BY
Kathleen Groll Connolly

AND
Paul M. Connolly

Lexington Books

D.C. Heath and Company/Lexington, Massachusetts/Toronto

This publication is designed to provide accurate and authoritative information in regard to the subject matter covered. It is sold with the understanding that the publisher is not engaged in rendering legal, accounting, or other professional service. If legal advice or other expert assistance is required, the services of a competent professional person should be sought.

— *From a Declaration of Principles jointly adopted by a committee of the American Bar Association and a Committee of Publishers.*

The authors are not engaged in delivery of legal services and advise that you review your policies and procedures with a competent legal advisor.

Library of Congress Cataloging-in-Publication Data

Connolly, Kathleen Groll.
    Competing for employees : proven marketing strategies for hiring and keeping exceptional people / by Kathleen Groll Connolly and Paul M. Connolly.
        p. cm.
    Includes bibliographical references and index.
    ISBN 0-669-21062-5
    1. Personnel management. 2. Selection of employees. 3. Employee morale. 4. Employee motivation. I. Connolly, Paul M. II. Title.
    HF5549.C7194   1991
658.3'11—dc20   90-24673
                                                                                           CIP

Published simultaneously in Canada.
Printed in the United States of America.
International Standard Book Number: 0–669–21062–5
Library of Congress Catalog Card Number: 90–24673

The paper used in this publication meets
the minimum requirements of American National Standard
for Information Sciences—Permanence of Paper
for Printed Library Materials, ANSI Z39.48-1984.

Year and number of this printing:

92 93 94 95 8 7 6 5 4 3 2

To our parents,

Joseph Connolly
Margaret Connolly
Dolores Groll

and especially William Groll,
who said that we must write a book.

Contents

List of Figures and Tables   ix

Acknowledgments   xiii

Introduction: The Need for Competitive Employment
    Strategy   xv

1. Marketing for Employers   1

2. Noncompetitive Employment   21

3. Be Definite   41

4. Know the Candidate's Vision of Employment   59

5. Use Market-Driven Recruiting   71

6. Sell Selectively   93

7. Treat New Employees Like New Customers   115

8. Be Retention Oriented   123

9. Measure "Customer" Satisfaction   139

10. The Competitive Employer   145

11. The Competitive Equation: A Self-Test   155

Appendix: Overview of Major Federal Employment
    Regulations   211

Bibliography   225

Index   229

About the Authors   233

List of Figures and Tables

Figures

I–1. External Forces—Internal Responses   xix

4–1. The Total Employment Purchase   60

5–1. The Target Applicant Pool   74
5–2. Positioning: Positive Differentiators   87
5–3. Positioning: Parity Points   88
5–4. Positioning: Negative Differentiators   89

10–1. External Forces—Internal Responses   146

Tables

I–1. Three Models of Management   xx

1–1. Employee Perspective on the Employment
Life Cycle   2
1–2. Employees as Buyers   6
1–3. Similarities of the Buying and Employment
Processes   9

2–1. The Costs to Wonderful Widgets of Losing
Joe Warmbody   26
2–2. Two Perspectives on Performance of Fundamental
Management Skills   34
2–3. Two Perspectives on Performance of Fundamental
Leadership Skills   35
2–4. The Competitive Impact of Eight Employer
Mistakes   38

3–1. Performance Requirements: Customer Service
      Representative   45
3–2. Motivational Requirements: Customer Service
      Representative   46
3–3. Environmental Requirements: Customer Service
      Representative   47
3–4. Wonderful Widgets and Joe Warmbody: How Good
      a Match?   49
3–5. Checklist: Performance Requirements   51
3–6. Checklist: Motivational Requirements   52
3–7. Checklist: Environmental Requirements   53
3–8. Summary Job Analysis   56

4–1. Total Employment Purchase: Tangible Job Features   61
4–2. Total Employment Purchase: Extended Features   62
4–3. Top Three Reasons for Leaving a Job   67

5–1. Basic Marketing Concepts as Applied to
      Employment   72
5–2. Applicant Locator: Where Can Applicants
      Be Found?   75
5–3. Wonderful Widgets Applicant Locator   76
5–4. Recruiting Media and Methods   78
5–5. Wonderful Widgets' Strengths and Weaknesses   84
5–6. Wonderful Widgets' Competitor's Strengths and
      Weaknesses   85

6–1. Comparison of Steps in the Selling and Hiring
      Processes   102

7–1. Orientation Topics   117
7–2. Most Commonly Made Orientation Mistakes   120

8–1. Major Components of High Employee Motivation   124
8–2. Management Behaviors Related to Effective
      Organizations   126
8–3. Determining Turnover Problems   134
8–4. The Telltale Signs of Turnover   136

9–1. Quickscan Employee Survey: Thirty Questions to
       Determine Where You Stand   141

10–1. How People Learn: Pointers for Effective Employee
        Training   150

A–1. Informal "Rules of Thumb" to Aid in the Determination of
       Employment Criteria for Job Knowledge
       and Skill   211
A–2. Knowledge and Skill Requirements for Wonderful Widgets'
       Customer Service Representative   212

Acknowledgments

We'd like to thank the people who helped us complete this book.

It is a difficult job to review an unfinished manuscript. A number of our friends, relatives, and business acquaintances did that for us. Their insights kept us on track. For their time, willingness and ideas, we thank: Vilma Allen, Gerry Boyan, Joe Connolly, Don Cowie, Robert Dugan, Charlotte Randolph Featherstone, Cynthia Groll, Norma Blacke Ocansey, Jean Powell Kirnan, Gordon Simerson, Diane Wentworth, and Peter Wentworth.

A number of people gave us their opinions and insights during interviews. Many of them are quoted in the book. Though others are not, their opinions and information were equally valuable. We'd like to thank all of them: Beth Anrig, Bob Chapman, Tom Conners, Jeannie D'Ambrosio, Anne Davenport, Patricia Denne, Dick Esser, John Fasolo, Trish Graf, Lyle Kishbaugh, Charles Lubner, Victor Meena, Charles Murphy, Debbie Oliver, Susan Palmer, Robert Rosenthal, Robert Saxton, Frank Scalia, Maureen Shannon, Roseanne Shegirian, Eileen Smith, and Gary Will.

We'd like to thank Bob Craig, who provided several invaluable referrals. Our thanks go also to Peter Eder, who provided the referral to our publisher.

Finally, our thanks to Lexington Books whose commitment to the publication of this book makes it possible for us to reach our readers.

Introduction:
The Need for Competitive
Employment Strategy

T wentieth-century theorists did not invent management. Management began with the master-slave relationship. For many centuries, masters owned slaves. Eventually, ownership gave way to various contractual arrangements, such as master-apprentice. Most of these arrangements heavily favored the master's right to control the worker.

Some would say the master-slave management model still manifests itself in management behavior, even though it is no longer found in our theories. Much of this thinking gave way in the last hundred years or so to a more benevolent form. This newer relationship resembles that of parent and child.

The parent-child model, like the earlier version, assumes that the manager knows more than the employee and that the manager has more control. Under this arrangement, however, management concerns itself with the welfare of the "child." To varying degrees, employers and their managers take care of the worker's training, health-care requirements, career growth, social status, retirement plans and sense of job security. The essential parent-child assumption is that "if you're a good child, you get to keep your job."

The parent-child model characterized many companies' unwritten employment contracts for the past seventy years. In the 1980s, it began to crumble.

For the employer's part, the parent-child model represented a contract that couldn't be upheld under the business conditions of the times. External forces were among the antagonists to the parent-child model: acquisition and divesture wars, international competition, and the need to serve up quarterly dividends. The final nails in the coffin of employer loyalty to "childlike" employees were driven in when AT&T and IBM, the bastions of lifetime employment, downsized and delayered.

Social forces also strain companies' abilities to practice a "parental" attitude today. Forty years ago their unwritten commitment was to provide lifetime employment to people who remained in good standing. Corporations now find themselves being asked to provide a variety of services to workers. The trends that make these services necessary affect so broad a cross section of the population that employers find them difficult to ignore. They include:

1. *At-home considerations.* Single parenthood, dual-career demands, child care, and elder care leave many a worker strapped for time and energy. As a result, employees are asking their companies for various forms of support for family responsibilities.

2. *Substance abuse problems.* Companies that use pre-employment drug testing report that between eight and fifteen percent of applicants fail these tests. No one really knows how many existing employees there are whose energies are being sapped daily by drug and alcohol problems. Those most familiar with the problem can only report that the answer is many. Companies thus find themselves dealing with this issue.

3. *Transportation difficulties.* The desire to work closer to home and avoid grueling commutes is driving many people to home offices, smaller cities, and other means of avoiding highly congested areas. Companies are increasingly asked by employees for the freedom to work at home for one or more days per week and, in some cases, to telecommute. In other cases, companies actually provide transportation to the work location.

This list—and its many ramifications—goes well beyond the set of concerns that even the most "parental" of corporations was ever prepared to handle.

From the employees' side, many can now demand equal status and view their employment as a type of partnership. Why has this happened? Some would say it was a temporary phenomenon of the 1980s economic expansion.

In the opinions of most demographers and human resources professionals, however, the answer is broader. A recent survey of human resources people, for instance, found 85 percent of them still concerned with labor and skills shortages—despite current economic troubles.[1]

Several factors fuel the long-term change:

1. *The Baby Boom/Baby Bust.* The baby boom/baby bust has unbalanced the labor supply. Demographers claim that this situation is unlikely to change for many years.

2. *The Skills Shortage.* Jobs are "skilling up"—that is, they are requiring more training and learning ability on the part of job holders. This puts a premium on the services of trained—or trainable—people.

3. *Increasing Diversity in the Workforce.* Workforce diversity challenges old assumptions about management—in all of its many phases. From recruiting and hiring through compensation and performance appraisal, culturally diverse worker populations have different employment preferences, communications styles, and work habits. In short, workforce diversity demands attention.

Aside from these trends, which are based in demographics, other factors fuel worker restlessness.

The high cost of living raises the ante for workers' services. In particular areas of the country, the cost of housing alone forces workers to constantly seek higher wages. Some are also concerned with the high costs of commuting. These concerns contribute to high employee turnover and a low sense of stability.

There is also a high perceived personal cost of employment. There is a broad social trend toward "having a life" outside of work. If work interferes, many people conclude that work should adapt to their personal needs—not the other way around. After all, they feel, there is no more employer loyalty.

The net effect of these and other changes is that the parent-child management model has lost utility and credibility. As with actual parents and children, growing up is hard on both. It's hard for the parent to let go, and it's a brave new world for the child.

The list of social forces at work today could go on. Perhaps the most important question relates to their implications: What will replace the parent-child management model? And what should the concerned employer do?

We see several reactions on the part of employers. Unfortunately the two most commonly used tactics provide only short term answers to what is a long term problem:

1. *Work longer hours.* This response is particularly common among small businesses, according to a 1987 study done for the Small Business Administration. Owner/entrepreneurs and their families compensate for worker shortages by working longer hours themselves.[2]

2. *Pay more money.* According to a study of member firms of the Society for Human Resources Management (formerly American Society of Personnel Administrators), the most common method of attracting applicants and retaining employees is to raise wages. That single approach is used by 58 percent of all respondents to the survey, who consist of both large and medium-size companies. This action not only raises costs for these firms, but it also raises the ante for smaller firms.[3]

Both solutions have very real limits. If you would do more than react, you must look for other strategies. Your strategy options fall into seven categories:

1. Integrated compensation strategies (beyond simple increases)
2. Training
3. Alternative staffing approaches
4. Technology as a supplement or complement to your work force
5. Management of workforce diversity
6. Creative use of geography
7. Competing for the right people more effectively, both before and after hiring

Many respected academicians and practitioners have written extensively about the first six strategies listed above, but we have

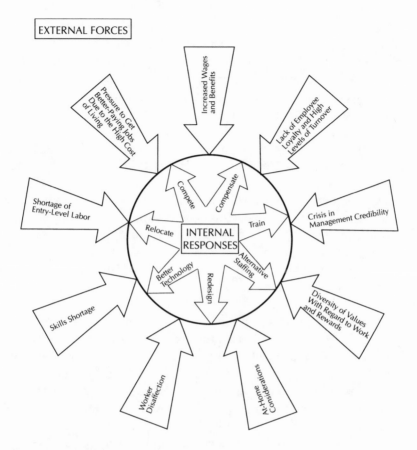

Figure I–1. *External Forces—Internal Responses*

rarely seen a discussion of the seventh. That one, then, is our focus here—an approach to effective employment competition. It requires no special tools. In fact, you already have the tools at your disposal. These tools are relatively cost-free and accessible to all. They are borrowed from your marketing department.

Competitive employment means you *know that employees are, at various points in the employment relationship, a type of customer.* What we call competitive employment in this book is a set of techniques, but above all it is the result of an attitude. It is an attitude that says you will work to earn the right to do business with your employees.

Competitive employers understand that people have diverse preferences, just as buyers in a marketplace do. Competitive employers acknowledge the decision-making processes of candidates and employees. Competitive employers try to grasp the implications of employees' varying personal agendas and to use that understanding to full advantage in the employment and management processes.

Their reward is a fundamentally different type of human resources relationship, a relationship that is adult-to-adult rather than adult-to-child.

The competitive employer understands and accepts that he or she alternates in roles of customer and supplier with employees. Throughout this book, we'll explore the implications of this constant shifting of roles.

Look at these three assumptions which characterize typical customer-supplier partnerships:

- Both customer and supplier must earn the right to the relationship. The supplier earns the right by delivering satisfactory (or even better, excellent) goods and services. The customer earns the right by paying for the goods and services.

  In an increasingly competitive world, smart customers help suppliers serve them by clarifying how the suppliers' products and services will be used. By doing so, the customer establishes the possibility for a deeper level of support from the supplier.

  Informed suppliers, who are close to the design and capabilities of their products and services, can help their customers by adapting and improving them for use in specific circumstances.

- Customers and suppliers each have the right to redefine their needs and directions. This may or may not end the relationship, depending on their abilities to adjust to the new requirements.

  Either the customers or the suppliers can put an end to the partnership if the other does not perform to specifications or expectations.

Welcome to the age of the customer-supplier management relationship (see table I–1).

Table I–1
Three Models of Management

Master-Slave Model	Parent-Child Model	Customer-Supplier Model
Slave must obey or be punished.	Child is enticed with "carrots," punished with "sticks."	Partners negotiate the transaction as equals.
Employee must obey or be disciplined.	"Be a good employee and you get to keep your job."	Both parties must earn the right to continue with the relationship.

How This Book Can Help

A tight labor supply can be as much a result of competitive recruiting and management as of any external forces. Companies are now adopting competitive techniques in various ways. The real winners in this new world of employment, we believe, will be those who have well-planned, integrated employment strategies that respect the employee as a customer. To help you become one of these winners, we have summarized the attitudes of competitive employment into five general topics.

1. Competitive employers are *definite about their needs.* Competitive employers plan their job descriptions carefully. They link their hiring to their business strategies in multiple ways. They have a concept of their ideal candidates.

2. Competitive employers understand and respond to what *their ideal candidates seek in ideal employers.* This is much broader than simple features such as good compensation.

3. Competitive employers use *candidate-centered* and *employee-centered* communications. They find differences that make a positive difference to their target candidates and key employees.

4. Competitive employers are *selective* in hiring, but they also acknowledge that the selection process is a *service* to the employee. It provides the candidate with sufficient insight to make an informed decision. Their hiring process more resembles the

establishment of a partnership than the simple process of selecting a worker.

5. Competitive employers are *retention-oriented*. They try to keep the right people. They know that the best defense against a tight labor and skills market is low turnover.

The chapters follow the progression of these five points, after a look at marketing—and its antithesis—for the employer.

Recognizing that you need to combine these five points with alternative approaches, chapter 10 briefly addresses training, staffing approaches, technology and geography.

If you're wondering how much competition for the right people affects you, go to the last chapter (Chapter 11—The Competitive Equation). This checklist will help you pinpoint your status, as well as show how well positioned you are to meet future employment challenges.

Finally, the bibliography refers you to important works on these subjects.

The discussions in this book will help you to:

1. Find your competitive strengths and weaknesses as an employer.

2. Understand the "buying psychology" of your employees.

3. Determine whether the employment problems you're facing are internal and controllable—or external and uncontrollable.

4. Develop specific recruiting, interviewing, and retention strategies for managing in a tight labor and skills market by brainstorming creative action options, ones that go beyond simple salary increases.

5. Find ways to break down company-internal resistance to the changes that will make you more competitive.

Competitive employment is a way of looking at recruiting and management. Used in combination with other strategies—compensation, training, alternative staffing, technology and geography—you will find yourself not only a more competitive employer but a more competitive business.

Notes

1. Right Associates, "The Checkoff," survey reported in *Wall Street Journal*, August 28, 1990.
2. See Douglas Brown, Implications of the Declining Supply of Entry Level Workers for Small Firms, Small Business Administration, (Washington, D.C., July 10, 1987) 31–43.
3. See Society for Human Resources Management, 1988 ASPA Labor Shortage Survey, (Alexandria, Va.: Society for Human Resources Management, 1988), 29.

1

An Introduction to Marketing for Employers

Customers—almost every businessperson knows a thing or two about how to get them and keep them. Everyone certainly knows how to be one.

As an employer, you may be wondering, "How do I get the right people to fill my job openings, stay with my company, and apply themselves to the work at hand?" If so, you are stating a basic marketing problem. In the following pages, you can apply what you yourself already know about being a customer and a supplier to the problem of employment.

Employees have been taught for years to market themselves to employers. But employers are only just beginning to learn to do the same. The sooner you accept employment as a two-way buying process, the sooner you can employ market-driven recruiting and management techniques.

Question: If this is the customer-supplier era of management, who is the customer and who is the supplier?

Answer: Your company, as an employer, will be *both* customer and supplier at different times. Under the traditional ways of thinking, you were in a buyer's market, with all the rights, power and problems that role brings. This point of view produces a company-centered orientation toward all aspects of management, from interviewing through termination. In the emerging world of employees-as-customers, you're also a supplier to your employees. Your management practices are actually a service to them, in that your management provides the environment in which people can perform their work.

Under a more equal relationship, employees are asserting their right to evaluate their employers. This manifests itself in the language they use, the attitudes they take and their commitment to the work. Table 1–1 looks at the employment relationship in the language of the job holder.

Table 1–1
Employee Perspective on the Employment Life Cycle

1. "I have employment choices."
2. "I hear about a company."
3. "I evaluate the company in terms of what's important to me."
4. "I choose to work for a company."
5. "I have many questions about the job and the company, most of which I figure out during the first few weeks on the job."
6. "I cooperate—or don't cooperate—with company management."
7. "I evaluate my insurance, vacation, and other employment benefits."
8. "I continue to have a choice about employment."
9. "I choose to stay with or to leave the company."

These are the terms now being used by an employee who is recruited ("I think I found a great place to work"), hired ("They made me an offer and I've accepted it"), managed ("I work for this guy in the telemarketing department who is pretty demanding"), motivated ("But he really knows what he's doing, gives us his support, and really seems to care") or mangled ("And he's a real jerk who thinks people are machines"), fired ("I'm going to sue") or accepts the offer of another job ("I couldn't take it anymore"). Any situation looks very different when seen from the different perspectives of employer and employee.

If employees are customers, they are not very satisfied ones. For years, researchers have pointed out the general lack of happiness among hourly workers. More recently, salaried workers' satisfaction with their management has dipped to similar lows. Some see it as a crisis of management credibility. Surveys of professional, technical, and management workers increasingly reveal disillusionment and lack of buy–in.[1]

The Crisis in Management Credibility

"American business leadership has lost some credibility with employees," says Lyle Kishbaugh, a twenty-year veteran of the human resources field. Currently Vice President-Human Resources for Cartier International, Kishbaugh offers these observations on the future of employee-employer relations:

1. *No sense of loyalty to the employer.* "People have justifiably decided that there's no value in employer loyalty," he says. "That was an unwritten contract, but it was a contract nonetheless. It's been violated by employers everywhere."

2. *Less sense of career.* "People now have more a sense of being on assignment—and one that won't last very long at that," says Kishbaugh. "They've been told that their promotions will be tougher to get and that they're going to have to find fulfillment by taking on more responsibility while staying in place."

3. *Employers will have fewer employees.* "I'm predicting that employers will contract out more and more work. This has serious implications for training and for quality assurance. Temporary workers can't feel the investment in a project that a long-term employee does."

As a result of these trends, "The average manager spends 60 percent of his or her time working, 20 percent worrying and 20 percent looking out for the next job."

"It's the best of times and the worst of times," he adds. "During a period of full employment, there has been a hidden unseen market of 'underemployed' people. A lot of people have been dislocated, but are still on payrolls, actively looking for jobs as good as what they had. They simply can't be counted. There are just an unknown number of people in this situation."

The Value of Marketing in an Employment Context

Sales and marketing people expect their customers to compare their products with the competitor's products. But the average hiring manager, even a sales and marketing manager, is not accustomed to workers and recruits doing the same. Thus, their responses to the new competitive employment environment rarely seem to take advantage of the many lessons that can be learned from market competition.

Marketers who plan competitive strategies use a few basic principles:

1. Understand a customer's perceived needs.

2. Understand a customer's perceived options—in other words, understand the competition, both direct and indirect.

3. Implement an approach that earns the right to do business with the customer. This means the creation of the right products, with the right services, the right reputation, and the right price. The work takes place not only before the sale, but afterward as well.

Contrast these attitudes with typical company attitudes towards staff members. Selection processes, for one thing, are typically company-centered. These are the steps followed in traditional selection and hiring processes. Compare the steps with those of the marketing manager:

1. Identify what skills and abilities the company needs from the employee.

2. Recruit and screen applicants on basis of the skills and abilities they offer the company.

3. After a favorable review, check the applicant's references, make an employment offer, and handle the administrative details of employment.

4. Entrust the new employee's manager with full responsibility for providing initiation, training, coaching, and motivation.

5. Review the employee based on his or her ongoing match with the company's immediate needs.

This traditional approach to employment reflects *a buyer's mentality*. It is viable when a company is in a buyer's market. But problems arise when you operate with *buyer's attitudes* in a *seller's market*.

Today, whether you know it or not, you compete with other buyers for the best employees. Moreover, after you have hired, you compete with other priorities for the employee's attention, energy, and drive. Yet despite the increasing necessity for employers to deal with employees competitively, the tendency of most employers is not to examine their buyer's mentality. Instead, they continue within it and even shop harder. They speed up their administration and processing of recruits. They lament the lack of "work ethic" in the work force. They complain that other employers pirate their companies. They advertise in more places, use more headhunters, and increase the number and pace of their selection activities.[2]

Unfortunately, such increased activity raises the cost of doing business, and can eventually undermine a company's overall competitiveness.

Employment as a Buying Process

The familiar language of buying and selling is often used in management circles. Managers talk about people accepting ideas and methods by saying they "buy into" them. Every manager has heard and probably made these kinds of comments:

"We've got to get employee buy-in."

"Do you think they'll buy this new way of doing things?"

"Maybe we'd better sell them on it before we do it."

"I'm shopping that idea around."

It shouldn't be too hard, then, for managers to shift perspectives and see that candidates and employees themselves use some selling and purchasing language. The resemblances are plain (see table 1–2).

Whether you look at hiring, at management, or at job hunting, mutual decision making takes place throughout employment relationships. In many respects, the decision-making process resembles a buying process. Yet, put in the employment context, most of us don't act in relation to potential employees as we would to customers.

Table 1–2
Employees as Buyers

Employee's Statement	Marketer's Translation
"They offered a higher salary."	This product had a better price.
"They have terrific benefits."	This product had more or better features than other, similar products.
"The people seem very friendly."	The salespeople were good at maintaining a customer focus.
"I like the offices."	The shopping environment is pleasant. I feel comfortable there.

Marketers often worry about their failures to fulfill the promises they make to customers. Customer satisfaction is a key marketing measure. Yet we rarely transfer this logic to employer-employee relations. We often expect employees to just "be patient and wait." If they take their business elsewhere, we say it was inevitable, it was their fault, and so on. Yet, turnover has a real and measurable cost—just as lost sales have a real and measurable cost.

A good model for looking at the employee or candidates purchasing process can be found in the marketing field. In the textbook sense, any purchase process has six major steps:

1. awareness of a need
2. search for information
3. evaluation of alternatives
4. decision-making
5. postpurchase reactions
6. repurchase

Understanding all these steps is important, because each of them has implications for your employment approach in the customer-supplier context.

Awareness of a Need

Every buying process begins with someone's awareness of a need, whether large or small. "I need to go grocery shopping" may be different in scale from "I need a new job," but the basic problem is the same. Once a need is felt, the person searches for resolution.

Information Search

The search for information about possible purchases may be very simple or very prolonged and complex. "I'll go to the neighborhood market" is a simple conclusion one may reach after reviewing the available local stores. The search for a job is rarely as simple as the search for a grocery, but it contains many of the same elements.

When potential buyers need to make a purchase decision they research their alternatives. Thus, the top priority of sales managers and advertising professionals—and grocery store owners—is to educate us about the alternatives they represent. They want to "be there" on the day we make our buying decisions. Tools they use to do this come under the heading of marketing communications. Similarly, in hiring new employees, you need to "educate" potential recruits about your company and job openings. If the right people are hard to find and keep, your job openings and your company need to "be there" when the right people consider their options and make their decisions.

Evaluation of Alternatives

Fulfilling a buying need usually involves reviewing the alternatives. In making a complex decision, such as the decision to take a new job, a buyer is likely to research, compare, and question. The buyer may weigh the compromises that one alternative requires in contrast to another. It may be a time of tension, low trust of the seller, and the buyer may desire to "get it over with quickly."

Decision Making

Making a decision to accept a particular job is psychologically similar to making the decision to buy a particular product. It is an uncomfortable state, in which one must abandon some alternatives in favor of others. It is also likely to be a time when trust of the seller is low, and the desire to "get it over with" may be high.

Postpurchase Behavior

Immediately after making a purchase, a buyer is very conscious of the decision he or she has made. "Did I do the right thing?" "Can this backfire?" "Did they tell me the truth?" People who have made a major decision, like a job choice, experience such uncertainties in magnified form. A bad experience with the decision soon after it has been made, while the buyer is still in a sensitive stage, can lead to long-term failure in the partnership. This is a time when the new buyer wants to enjoy the new purchase. If the buyer has a bad experience now, or if the salesperson handles the situation improperly, the result can be that a time of potential enjoyment becomes a time of high frustration.

Repurchase

Ultimately, a buyer decides whether he or she would buy the same product again. Employees make a similar decision every day. They buy into their employment, and give it effort, commitment, and attention every day.

Employment is a purchasing process, and associated tangible and intangible needs are a part of its mix. Your acknowledgment of this is central to competitive employment. Recognizing that you are in a competition, you must be ready to compete in three general time frames during your company's relationship with a candidate or employee:

1. *During recruitment.* This is the time of the most obvious competition. It is measured by the direct expense of recruiting activities and the successes achieved.

2. *During employment.* You compete to earn the full productive participation of your workforce, against their personal distractions and other pursuits. This is not an easily measurable area of competition. If you win in it, you keep your most motivated people. If you lose in it, your costs usually include the lost productivity of slow disillusionment.

3. *When another opportunity arises.* At the time when valued employees weigh their continued employment, you compete to

earn their continued tenure and prevent an expensive loss to yourself. You may not know you're in competition until an employee resigns.

Table 1–3 shows how the purchasing process for shoppers is very similar to both the hiring process for employers and the job-hunting process for workers.

In a tight labor and skills market, employers can benefit by understanding the buying psychology of their most attractive target candidates and their existing employees.

Table 1–3
Similarities of the Buying and Employment Processes

Steps of the Buying-Decision Process	Shopper Shopping for Goods and Services	Employer Hiring People	Employee Job-Hunting
1. Awareness of a Need	Put it on the shopping list	Create a job opening and determine who is most likely to succeed	Start reading papers and talking to friends
2. Information Search	Where is it sold?	Where are likely applicants?	Where are they hiring?
3. Evaluation	Compare the alternatives	Interview the applicants	Go to the interviews
4. Decision	Buy	Hire	Accept offer
5. Post-purchase	Did I make a good decision?	Did we make a good decision?	Did I make a good decision?
6. Repurchase	Will I buy that product again?	Will I give him/her a raise or promotion?	Do I want to keep this job?

Resistances to Marketing

Throughout this book, we apply marketing concepts to employment. Some people won't find this perspective useful, appealing, or in some cases even ethical.

When those who agree with the competitive employment approach propose that managers in their company adopt it, these managers may not be ready to accept the steps to competitive

employment. Some may not be convinced that they need to compete. Some will feel threatened by the power that it seemingly
hands to the employee. Some will feel that the practice of marketing itself is unethical, knowing it only by two of its least attractive,
most often abused aspects: high pressure sales and hype. Still
others will resist the notion of competing for the right people just
because it represents a change.

In fact, if you would have your organization compete more
effectively for the right people, you must be prepared to change
managers' attitudes. In marketing parlance, you'll be facing *sales
objections* from managers. The newer and more innovative the
product concept, the greater the change that is required of the
customer—and the bigger the sales objection is likely to be. Like
marketers, agents of organizational change face sales objections.

Why is this so?

1. *News of labor and skill shortages gives a negative message
   to managers.* Is there any good news in a shortage, after all,
   unless you're on the supplier side? A shortage means higher
   wages. It means working harder to find people. It means
   uncertainty about your ability to find a qualified person at
   all. "Will I have to settle for just a 'warm body' to get this
   job filled?" The ultimate negative, of course, is that people,
   unlike inanimate objects, have an ongoing freedom of
   choice.

2. *Competition is a relatively new concept in the human
   resources arena.* Most of what we know as competition
   takes place in the form of measurable events. A game is
   won, a sale is made, a product line achieves top market
   share. By contrast, the results of good human resources
   management are much less measurable. They are often
   qualitative rather than quantitative.

3. *The results of good employee selection and good management usually occur long periods of time later.* What
   marketers would call the "win" is not an obvious and
   immediate event, but the result of a process. Successful processes are more difficult to appreciate than successful
   events because the feedback is subtle and relatively slow. As
   time passes and events intertwine, the effects of particular
   actions are obscured.

Does It Pay to Invest in Human Resources?
The Human Resources Effectiveness Index

Many businesspeople are from Missouri when it comes to making investments in human resources. "Show me," they say, "that human resources investments pay back." Because of this, the lack of good measurements has worked against the acceptance of many proposals for improved human resource management.

Several researchers have recently addressed the lack of measurements, however. In his Ph.D. dissertation, Jack J. Phillips, executive vice president of human resources at Secor Bank in Birmingham, Alabama, broke new ground towards a "human resources effectiveness index." He studied seventy-six organizations that employ a total of 521,466 people. Using six measures of human resource performance and four measures of organizational effectiveness, Phillips found many positive relationships between the two. The organizational measures included revenue per employee, assets divided by employee costs, operating income divided by employee costs, and operating income divided by stockholders' equity.

Some of Phillips' findings:

- Training and development investment is positively correlated with measures of organizational effectiveness such as revenue and return on equity.

- As human resource management expense increases (the expenses related to staffing and operating the human resource department itself), every other organizational effectiveness measure increases as well.

- As employee turnover increases, the measures of organizational effectiveness decrease.

- As employee absenteeism increases, effectiveness measures decrease.

Phillips' work is based on a larger measurement project being conducted by the Society of Human Resource Managers (formerly ASPA) and the Saratoga Institute. The project aims to collect standardized human resources performance data that allows companies to compare their performance with others.[3]

4. *Specific human resource competitors are rarely identified.*
    Instead, "the competition" for employees remains a vague
    generalization, such as "other stores" or "other manufac-
    turers." Only occasionally, when one company begins to
    "pirate" employees from another, is a clear employment
    competitor identified.

Does It Pay to Invest in Human Resources?
Forecasting the Financial Benefits

Numbers are the traditional language of business, yet human
resource development has traditionally resisted quantification. "As a
result, the average businessperson views it as peripheral, out of the
mainstream," says Richard Swanson, a professor and director at the
University of Minnesota's Training and Development Research Center.

Swanson and coauthor Deane Gradous show how to quantify
the value of structured training in their book, *Forecasting the
Financial Benefits of Human Resource Development.* Their methods
of deriving and presenting costs and benefits help the practitioner
use the universal language of business.

"In the early 1980s, a renaissance in business thinking provided
incentive to look at people development as an investment," Swanson
says. "However, we still need to address the dilemma of selecting one
program investment versus another."

Swanson and Gradous illustrate how returns on competing
training and development approaches are quantified, much as
returns on other investments are quantified.

They outline an approach for calculating the value of performance improvement:

- Units of work performance must be defined.
- Performance levels must be known—both those that occurred
  before the developmental program and those expected as a result
  of the program.
- Value must be assigned to the increased units of performance.

From these, the value of performance improvement can be quantified and justified on a business basis.

"Organizations are looking for partners in change, internal
venture capitalists," says Swanson. "By speaking the same language
as the rest of the business team, the human resource professional can
present programs from a bottom-line benefits point of view."[4]

Removing Reasons to Say No to Change

No effective salesperson would ever tell a prospect who's just voiced a buying objection, "You're wrong." Likewise, people trying to bring about organizational change won't find it a useful technique, either—particularly with managers from the "old school."

To overcome their resistance, take two steps:

1. *You must first accept that you are in the role of organizational salesperson.* Your "commission" on the sale is to reduce resistance and to align your organization more closely with today's business environment. In the long run, this will make your job easier and, hopefully, your company more successful.

2. *Build a relationship with the resister.* If he or she knows, trusts, and respects you, your approach will be towards gaining agreement on the issue at hand. If the resister doesn't know, trust, or respect you, there's a great deal of ground work to be done before the issue can be successfully addressed.

Sales professionals know that sales objections are based on a buyer's perception. These perceptions form reasons to say no in the buyer's mind. The best salespeople become expert at "burying false objections" and building value by working to change perceptions. In other words, they attempt to remove all reasons for a prospect to say "no."

Let's look at how these sales techniques work in the following examples of resistance:

*Resistance 1: "Why Should I Change the Way I Work
with Secretaries (or Other Difficult to Recruit Positions)?"*

Change often represents a perceived loss of services without a corresponding tangible improvement. The classic example is manager who expects to have coffee served. The organizational salesperson has two options:

1. *Educate the manager on the benefits of change.* For example, the salesperson could argue that peers might see the

buyer as a more effective manager. Subordinates might see the buyer as a "good person to work for." Upper management might see the manager as using a scarce resource (that is, a high turnover group) more effectively. Another approach is to show that the position will be filled less frequently. This reduces the time that must be spent on training replacements.

2. *Find alternative ways of letting managers have their coffee.* For instance, offer to buy them a coffee pot. Maybe cafeteria personnel can be hired to deliver coffee.

Of course, there are a number of more forceful options such as telling the manager who is resisting to stop or getting the resister's pay raise tied to various changes in the way he or she behaves.

Resistance 2: "We Can't Increase Recruiting Budgets. There's No Money for It."

Buyers look at costs. The salesperson's job is to demonstrate *value* —of which costs are only one component. Value is the perceived relationship between costs and benefits. To sell the resister on value, you must work with his or her perceptions.

The organizational salesperson must understand the specific benefits that make a difference to the organizational customer whose behavior they hope to change. Selling the wrong benefits produces, at best, indifference to your requests.

Resistance 3: "I Don't Want to Save That Employee. I Can't Wait for Him or Her to Leave."

It's often simpler to let people leave than it is to learn to work with them. The speaker here is really saying that he or she doesn't know how to handle employee problems (or problem employees). To this manager, it looks easier to replace problems rather than to assume responsibility as a manager.

Talking about the costs of turnover probably won't overcome the resistance here. To really overcome this objection, the resister will need to increase his or her management skills—and confidence.

This manager may also be reacting to weaknesses in the overall personnel policies at the company. Unclear policies regarding "firing offenses," absenteeism, and other areas may make the resisting manager feel that it's better to wait for turnover than to take a stand on a shaky policy.

Resistance 4: "We Don't Need to Use More Headhunters. The Newspaper Always Worked for Me When I Was Recruiting."

Some people genuinely don't understand a valid need because of their frame of reference. The good organizational salesperson will acknowledge a manager's frame of reference—then proceed to supply data that offers a new one. In the case of this resistance, perhaps internal statistics and certainly outside sources on the current costs of recruiting should be made available.

Resistance 5: "If That Employee Would Just Do His or Her Job, Things Would Be All Right."

When one human resources manager proposed an adult literacy program, she got this reaction to her proposal: "Managers thought we were covering up for poor recruiting and interviewing," she said. "If we in human resources would just do our jobs better, the company wouldn't need to offer literacy programs. They weren't convinced of a literacy problem in the population."

The resistance here is not simply an old-fashioned frame of reference. It is an objection to the way human resources is doing its job of serving the organization. It implies a "we-they" problem. The salesperson must first overcome the latter objection before the buyer will be willing to be reeducated. You might respond by saying, for example, "Okay. Is there anything you [we] can do which might help them do their job better?"

Resistance 6: "I Don't See What Difference It's Going to Make."

The objection as it is stated here may be different from the underlying objection. The resister objects because some larger issue will block success. This speaker may have one or two problems with change:

1. *He or she may doubt the organization's ability to change or cope with results of change.* So why bother to try? Any talk about the benefits of a new performance appraisal will go unheard until this sense of futility is addressed. Particularly in areas where change is complex, it is easy to doubt the impact of seemingly small actions.

2. *He or she may be afraid of the consequences of having to deal with employees in a more stringent manner.*

The salesperson has to smoke out the real objection before any progress will be made.

Resistance 7: "I'm Not in a Position to Change This."

The speaker here is declining ownership of a problem.

One professional told us, "My boss turns over secretaries at a rate of about two per year. I can see what the problems are, but I can't tell her. I keep quiet and do my job."

Another executive told us, "I really believe in training. But the boss just doesn't buy it. He'll let you send people to courses, but they come back to our old fashioned way of doing things and just get frustrated. What's the use?"

The resisters here may have either of two possible problems. One possibility is that they are avoiding responsibility, pushing the reasons for not changing onto another individual. A second possibility is that they're saying that the consequences of trying to change outweigh the potential benefits.

Resistance 8: "I Don't Have Time to Go to Programs on Managing a Diverse Work Force. What Do They Think I Do All Day?"

Change requires personal time and effort. People might agree a change is needed, but they may not see how they can spare the effort, given the other demands they face. They may also use "no time" as an excuse to avoid dealing with a deeper, less obvious objection—or one that isn't socially acceptable. ("I don't care about diversity—let 'them' conform to the rules.")

Lack of time is rarely a good excuse when making the desired change has clear priority. There is always time for the most important things. The above resister is saying that programs on diverse work forces aren't as important as other things he or she wants to do. The person may also be saying that programs of this sort lack top management support.

The salesperson has to find a way to relate the change to the buyer's priorities.

Resistance 9: "I'm Appalled at What Some of These Young People Expect."

Some managers believe in the "traditional" approach to career or job advancement, especially if they themselves were subjected to or ruled by it.

For instance, one senior manufacturing manager related with candor a feeling that others in his age group may share: "I got my first management job when I was thirty. To become a supervisor at that age was quite an achievement. Now, young people seem to feel it's their right to get into management within a year after they leave college. Personally, I'm offended by the attitude."

This manager has a personal prejudice because of the "way I did it." This prejudice is unlikely to change. But the salesperson can aim to get the resister to accept a new way of looking at the situation. For instance, you might discuss the idea that the language of job descriptions has changed. Thirty years ago, sanitation workers were called garbage men. Similarly, many of the positions that today carry a manager's title were, thirty years ago, described as administrator or supervisor positions. Try to build a bridge to the buyer's view of the world.

Resistance 10: "Don't Talk to Me about Pressure on People. Sales Are Down. We've Got to Fix That First."

Business distracts people with competing priorities and the necessity of maintaining day to day operations. In this case, the amount of pressure people are under seems a low priority compared with the business issues at hand.

The resister's statement creates an opportunity for the salesperson to show that the pressure has a relationship to sales. "If I could show you that reduced pressure would help you get your job done, would you be more interested?" Now the salesperson needs to be prepared to show how and why the proposed change will work. It's a good idea to have specific suggestions in mind, such as taking a small group of people and trying some new or improved approach. Otherwise, attention to high pressure or other problems will continue to take a back seat to perceived priorities.

Resistance 11: Objections to Marketing.

Some people object to marketing as such, knowing it as they do only by two of its least attractive aspects: high pressure sales and hype.

"Marketing Is Just a Lot of Hype." According to the dictionary, hype is advertising that achieves its ends through tricks and gimmicks. "Marketing hype," says Peter Eder, senior vice president at the Association of National Advertisers, "is the repetitive presentation of positive, partial information seemingly endorsed by seemingly authoritative sources."[5]

Why do people use hype? Eder, who has written extensively on the subject, explains that with hype, "Complex issues and ideas are often presented in a simplified and positively stated fashion. The information is presented to encourage early adopters to try something new, to make financial backers more willing to take a risk, to make that risk appear less severe."

He goes on to note that hype has both positive and negative sides. "Hype can lead to positive expectations. . . . From the negative view, however, a primary hazard has to be the possibility of misleading the audience as to the potential degree of success. Hype accepted as truth can cause incorrect decisions and expensive errors."

People are wary of hype because most of us can point to an instance in which it led to a purchasing mistake. Likewise, some may be wary of hype in the employment context because it can lead to employment mistakes. Just as hype can lead to angry customers who won't come back, so hype in the employment setting leads to distrust, expensive turnover, or even a lawsuit.

"Marketing Is Manipulative." The object of marketing is to stimulate buying behavior. Practiced honestly, it facilitates useful exchanges between buyer and seller. Some people, however, feel that marketing is manipulative because it uses powerful communications techniques that have the power to turn "wants" into "needs."

We've all been known to say, "I need an ice cream cone," "I need a better car," "I need to keep up with the latest fashions," "I need a hamburger." In truth, these are all "wants" that we experience with heightened anticipation as if they were really needs. To some extent, we may feel this way because of marketers' promotions.

Indeed, marketing tools can be and have been used to stimulate purchases that some view as objectionable. But they are also used to promote social service agencies, schools, environmental causes, better health practices, and many other things that have positive social benefits. They're used because they work.

In the wrong hands, marketing techniques can produce undesirable results. Used by the well-intentioned, they can provide a level of effectiveness that will help to add a measure of control in a largely uncontrollable situation.

In the next chapters, we'll look at the attitudes on which competitive employment is based. We'll contrast them with noncompetitive attitudes. If you would have your company accept these attitudes, be prepared to help it make the transition from traditional one-sided ways of thinking about employees. Everyone knows how a customer should be treated. Your job is to help your company see employees as a type of customer.

Notes

1. Robert Kelley, "Survey of Gold Collar Workers," press release, Carnegie Mellon University Department of Public Relations, (November 9, 1989).
2. See Society for Human Resources Management, 1988 ASPA Labor Shortage Survey, (Alexandria, Va.: Society for Human Resources Management, 1988), pp. 25–29.

3. Summarized from Jack J. Phillips, The Development of a Human Resources
   Effectiveness Index, (Ph.D. diss., University of Alabama, 1988. Available
   from UMI, 300 North Zeeb Road, Ann Arbor MI 48106). Further information also to be included in Phillips's forthcoming book, *Evaluating the
   Human Resources Function*, San Francisco: Jossey-Bass.
4. R. Swanson and D. Gradous, *Forecasting the Financial Benefits of Human
   Resource Development*, (San Francisco: Jossey-Bass, 1988).
5. Peter Eder, *The Use of Hype in Promoting Interactive Telecommunications*,
   (master's thesis, New York University, 1988).

2
*Non*Competitive Employment

M any noncompetitive employment practices are simply outdated practices that have been carried over by habit into the
new employment setting. To explore the fallacies that can occur
with these practices, we look first at an example—a composite of
real situations that we have seen through our consulting practice.
The case is that of Joe Warmbody, a customer service representative who is leaving the Wonderful Widgets Corporation.

Warmbody's unhappy departure embodies many aspects of a
tight labor and skills market. Angry after a brief period of employment, Joe Warmbody is ready to tell the world how bad an employer Wonderful Widgets is. He's had a rough tour there. He finds
another job after only a short search. He even increases his pay.

Wonderful Widgets' managers breathe a collective sigh of relief
at Joe's departure. The story shows how Wonderful Widgets made
some classic hiring errors in a tight labor and skills market.

What is wrong with this picture?

The Case of Joe Warmbody

Meet Joe Warmbody, former member of Wonderful Widgets Corporation's customer service department. After just eight months
with Widgets, he's found a new job at a higher salary.

"Let the Buyer Beware"

*Setting: Another day at Wonderful Widgets Corporation. We join the
human resources manager, Mary Jones, and Joe Warmbody. Joe and
Mary have just finished an exit interview. Things didn't work out
exactly as planned at his customer service department job.*
Mary: Well, Joe, the last thing we had to go over were your employee
benefits. Any questions?

Joe: No, I have no more questions.

Mary: When do you start your new job?

Joe: Tomorrow.

Mary: Okay, then, I think that's everything. We're sorry things didn't work out for you here with us. I'm sure I speak for everyone here at Wonderful Widgets, though, in wishing you the best. We hope you find whatever it is you want.

Joe: Right, Mary. I wish Wonderful Widgets the same.

Joe Warmbody's Point of View

Joe Warmbody had a lot of trouble with his job at Wonderful Widgets.

From his point of view, Wonderful Widgets' customers were a mistreated group. Many customers complained about the quality of Wonderful Widgets products and about delivery delays. As a customer service representative, he felt pressured by the company "not to give in" to customer requests. Yet he often found himself in agreement with customers and was unable to hold up the company point of view to them.

He had left his previous job—which in hindsight was a better one—when Widgets made him a salary offer he couldn't refuse. In fact, about the only good thing that happened to him at Wonderful Widgets was that he improved his salary. When he started talking to headhunters a few months after he joined, he set his price even higher than before.

Joe blames his manager, Ralph Raymond, for not supporting him. Ralph never dealt with Joe's questions very well. He never wanted to know "the details" of what Joe was doing, but he would get upset later when he found out those same details. Joe never had a clear idea of exactly what he was supposed to do. When things went right, Ralph didn't notice. When things went sour, Ralph was right there to point out Joe's errors.

Joe thinks to himself now, "I don't like to argue, and I don't like confrontation. I told them that. I have always liked working with customers, and I've been able to handle some difficult ones. But I can't do the job by myself."

Joe's first day on the job had consisted of some introductions around the department and being shown to his desk. For training, he was supposed to read the customer manuals and a departmental guidebook on handling customers' questions. During the first week, he got some instruction from another department member. After that, he was treated as if he'd been there for years. Problem was, he hadn't.

The employee newsletter had recently devoted a full page to an article entitled "The New Team Spirit." After eight months, Joe was pretty sure he would be waiting a very long time before he'd actually see any of this kind of spirit. His co-workers, he thought, wouldn't know teamwork if they saw it.

The job had been a real drain on Joe's energy. He had heard Wonderful Widgets was fast-paced. During the interview, he had asked about items like scheduling and overtime. Both Mary and Ralph had insisted that "we're adding staff so we can manage the workload better." All that had happened was that the workload increased. Joe then found out that *he* was the extra staff.

Joe began looking for a new job after his six-month review, when Ralph Raymond had said to him, "You've got to do a better job of supporting company policies." After that, Joe had talked to headhunters almost as much as he talked to customers. It took only a month to find his new job—and he is even going to enjoy another salary boost.

Warmbody has gladly warned his friends away from working for Wonderful Widgets. The people who talk to him wonder out loud, "Why would anyone want to work for them?"

"What a relief it is to be out of here," Warmbody almost screams as he leaves the parking lot for the last time. "I never should have joined them in the first place." Turning philosophical, he whispers to himself, "Let the buyer beware."

Wonderful Widgets' Point of View

Of course, there are at least two sides to any story. Ralph Raymond, customer service manager, also has some strong feelings about "the Joe Warmbody situation."

He interviewed Warmbody for a customer service position nine months ago, and he can't believe what happened. Warmbody must have lied when he said he liked customer service work. Joe hadn't been with Wonderful Widgets one month before he started pressing Ralph to "get off the phones."

At the interview, Ralph had asked Joe how he felt about handling difficult customers, and Joe had said it had "never been a problem" for him. Ralph explained that in Wonderful Widgets' industry, customers usually call when they have a crisis brewing on their hands. Their Widgets are key to critical manufacturing processes and customers can't tolerate downtime. Therefore, customers are often very disturbed when they call the customer service department. Joe had said he understood that, and he said in fact that it was something he was used to handling.

But from the very first day, Warmbody had been unable to uphold the company's policies. Joe was always trying to convince Ralph to compromise on a company policy or procedure to appease a customer. Warmbody is a pushover, Ralph thinks. He can't handle conflict. His idea of conflict resolution is to give the store away.

Ralph recalls that Mary Jones had gone out of her way to recruit Warmbody. Well, he had seemed the perfect candidate at the time. He must have lied during his interview with her, too.

Ralph gets a call from Mary Jones after Joe Warmbody leaves.

Mary: It's over, Ralph. Warmbody's out of here.
Ralph: Finally! What a relief! When can I expect a replacement?
Mary: Let's take one problem at a time. I don't have anyone for you yet. I'll get back to you as soon as I can. We had a few lined up after that job fair we attended, but they never showed up for their interviews. We'll keep trying.
Ralph: Well, look, I need somebody, anybody—except Warmbody, that is! See what you can do. Whoever we get is going to have to be able to hit the ground running, so no trainees.
Mary: I think I understand the kind of person you're looking for.
Ralph: Keep those applicants coming. We'll just have to plan on losing half of them every year. See if you can find a few who can stick it out with us longer, though.
Mary: I'll do what I can.

For her part, Mary Jones puzzles over how much harder recruiting has become recently. The high cost of living and employees' transportation problems are making her life tougher. Applicants now often lack the basic job skills that the average applicant used to have. Management doesn't realize how tough things have become. The harder she works, the less they seem to appreciate it. One manager has even suggested to her that she might be "losing her touch."

Mary knows that other human resource people in the region are also concerned about the generally declining quality of applicants. At Wonderful Widgets, basic standards have constantly been lowered, while starting wages have increased dramatically.

The management team is frustrated. Wonderful Widgets isn't getting the benefit of better worker productivity from the premium wages they pay. Worker mistakes have led to quality and delivery problems, and higher-than-average industry wages are creating price pressures.

Jones certainly doesn't want a repeat of the Warmbody situation, but now she's really in a spot. Raymond needs a new employee right away. Maybe she could tweak some applicant interest in this job opening by adding a few more dollars to the starting salary, she thinks. Management won't like it, but the customer service phones keep ringing, and angry customers are worse than upset managers. She wonders if the existing customer service representatives will demand that all CSRs be given raises to the level of the "starting wage" she's going to advertise. Well, maybe they won't catch it this time.

"What a relief. Joe Warmbody is gone," she whispers to herself.

She scans the recruitment ad she has used for the past few years:

Customer Service Representatives: Are You Good Enough to Join Our Top-Notch Team?

Wonderful Widgets Corp., the world's best maker of things people need, has an immediate opening for a motivated performer to join our hard-working, highly successful team. We need someone who is willing to work hard on challenging new projects. Only star performers need apply. We offer top pay for top performers, with salaries up to $35,700.

You will handle customers' needs for our worldwide client base. If you're tired of a mundane work environment, our hands-on, fast-moving environment might be for you. You must have three years of related experience. A college degree from a recognized institution is preferred but not required. Highly competitive salary and benefits, commensurate with experience.

Please, no visits or calls. Send your resumé to Wonderful
Widgets Corp., Employment Screening, Box 12, Central City,
USA.

Well, she thinks, the ad worked before. We'll just have to screen
more carefully this time. As she picks up the phone to convince
Ralph Raymond that they need to adjust the starting salary in her
advertisement, she whispers to herself: "Let the buyer beware."

What Went Wrong?

Wonderful Widgets and Joe Warmbody have been both victim and
villain in this case. They both failed in their employment partnership.

Wonderful Widgets, as the trustee of the employment partnership, had the responsibility to select carefully and manage effectively. The company made several key mistakes in this area.

Furthermore, the cost of this employment turnover is tangible.
From recruitment through termination, a conservative estimate of
the expenses associated with the mismatched hire of Joe Warmbody
are shown in table 2–1.

Table 2–1

The Cost to Wonderful Widgets of Losing Joe Warmbody

Original advertising campaign:	$ 750
Compensation and benefits, first two months:	5,850
Cost of new, expanded recruiting campaign:	900
Cost of first two months' compensation and benefits, with increase, of new replacement:	5,925
Total:	$13,425

Note: Of course there were additional intangible costs, such as management time, and lost productivity, which would make the cost even
higher. A two-month training period is assumed.

In this section, we look at some of the mistakes Widgets made
and begin to explore what it can do about them.

Wonderful Widgets' problem is that it lacks the attitudes of competitive employment.

1. It did not have a plan to find an "ideal" candidate.

2. It made a number of recruiting errors, most notably that of focusing on its own needs.

3. It made interviewing and selection errors.

4. It used compensation as an answer to problems that compensation cannot fix.

5. Its orientation practices are ineffective.

6. Its training is too informal given the performance expectations held by the manager.

7. Perhaps most important of all, it tolerates an ineffective manager, Ralph Raymond.

Joe Warmbody isn't blameless, either. Unfortunately for the employer, though, this is somewhat beside the point. Wonderful Widgets bears the brunt of the costs for the failure. Each point of its failure is explored in greater depth below:

Planning

Wonderful Widgets didn't define the type of person who would succeed in its work environment. This reduced its ability to attract and screen people who had a good chance of success. Their advertising used salary, the title of the job, and geography as the key descriptors by which applicants could prequalify their interest. Had the company better understood its own needs, it could have better prequalified its applicants for their potential "fit" with the work and company environment. It would also have interviewed applicants not only for their skills and motivation but for their adaptability to the sometimes-difficult customer service environment.

Recruiting

Can you imagine a marketing department running the following ad
for customers?

Customers Wanted:
Are You Good Enough to Buy from Us?

> Wonderful Widgets Corp., the world's best maker of things
> people need, has a product for a motivated customer who's good
> enough to buy from our hardworking, highly successful team. We
> need customers who are willing to work hard at using our
> challenging new products. We give every customer a different
> price, depending on their qualifications. Only experienced
> customers need apply.
>
> We are a very busy company, so please don't bother us in
> person or by telephone. Send your request to: Wonderful Widgets
> Corp., Customer Screening, Box 12, Central City, USA.

We can probably agree that such self-centered advertising as
this would be a waste of the advertiser's money. The likes of this
ad are rarely seen in the world of product marketing. Yet this unlikely
ad is the equivalent of much recruitment advertising, including
Wonderful Widgets' ad.

Wonderful Widgets' employment ad describes who the company is and what the company wants. The only solid job information it gives is the location, the job title, and the requirement of
three years' experience. It opens the door to numerous miscommunications, such as these:

1. It speaks in language that employers, not employees, love to
hear—"star performer," "highly motivated," "highly successful,"
and "team." Many employers delight in telling the world (and
their competitors) about the company's "hardworking team" and
"hands-on, fast-moving environment."

But potential employees are likely to have a different reaction.
They might read the same phrases as "working hard" or "overworked." They might find the entire ad full of company chest-
beating and self-congratulation.

Candidates and employees think about their employment in personal terms, but generally not in the language of management. "I heard or read about an opening. Sounds like it might match my skills or interests," they may think, or "Sounds like it's closer to home." The wording of this advertisement, then, fails to communicate what the candidates are seeking in employment.

2. *Most* people think of themselves as "motivated" or even as "star performers." The recruiting-ad writer may think that top performers "know who they are" and will come forward, but we would suggest that performers of all quality levels—including those at the bottom—might well think this ad is speaking to them. Few people think of themselves as poor performers. It's human nature to attribute performance problems to someone or something other than oneself.

3. "Top salaries for top performers" tells the potential applicant nothing about how that top salary of $35,700 is really achieved. High pay is an attractant that does little to qualify the sincerity of applicants' interest in the job.

4. This ad doesn't describe any of the job, work environment, or company values by which the most desirable applicants could properly distinguish Wonderful Widgets from many other companies.

5. "Please, no visits or calls" works against whatever motivation to action was created through the ad. Most advertisers, by contrast, try to motivate an immediate purchase, and they do all they can to make it easy as possible for the customer to buy rather than obstruct a purchase.

Such inappropriate recruiting communications as these can increase an employer's problems in a tight labor or skills market. These communications include the company's advertisements, what current and former employees say about the company, and the messages given by the recruiters. If the communications are negative, the company could be creating its own employment competition.

Interviewing and Selection

Wonderful Widgets' screening and interviewing are driven largely by the hiring manager's intuitions. Since it didn't define its hiring standards ahead of time, this is hardly surprising. Ralph Raymond always leans toward his "gut feelings."

"I know a good person when I see one," think interviewers of the Ralph Raymond type. "I can size someone up very accurately in just a few minutes."

This type of interviewers' unspoken assumption is that his or her "gut feelings" can't be wrong. But while interviews can be very effective, such poor interviewing techniques as this result in interviews that are poor predictors of actual job performance.

The fact is that interviewers generally overestimate their own ability to "read people." When a new hire's performance isn't as expected, interviewers rarely blame their own powers of perception. Instead, they think the person consciously misled them or that a reference didn't warn them. They look to some external circumstance instead of their own interviewing technique.

Both Mary Jones and Ralph Raymond, for instance, failed to listen carefully to Joe Warmbody at their interviews with him. "I'm a team player," he said. If they had done further probing, they would have learned that Joe is the kind of person who needs a cooperative, low-tension, quiet environment. He needs time to think and plan.

A quiet person like Joe would be irritated by Wonderful Widgets' noisy customer service environment. Someone who performs a job well at one company may be totally unsuited to doing the same job at another company. Job environments differ greatly from one company to another, even among companies in the same industry. Mary and Ralph missed this point as well. They focused instead on the idea that an easygoing person would be a good addition to their highly stressed department. They didn't want to train the new CSR, and Warmbody's previous experience seemed to fit their needs. Both these expectations backfired, and Joe felt abused. His needs couldn't be met by the environment they offered.

Even if a company interviews carefully, the pressure to hire is sometimes so strong that the company feels forced to make major hiring compromises. Unless you have a plan to compensate for the compromise you make, this is exactly the wrong thing to do.

While well intentioned, such compromises can produce negative side-effects. Additional management time and resources may be needed. Established employees may lose productivity. Indeed, established employees can get a poor impression from the company's lowered hiring standards. They might feel their skills are less valued. Other side-effects include increased errors, increased amount of rework, and lower overall product or service quality.

Compensation

Labor shortages increase wage and benefit levels. If you don't provide higher wages and benefits, your employment competition down the street very well might. But simple wage and benefit increases raise the ante without helping the business unless you also have a plan to improve productivity, reduce other costs, or increase revenues.

Wonderful Widgets pays well, but why? What impact does it have on their business? Mary Jones's reply is, "We have to pay more. Everybody else is." She is correct, but she and her management should be addressing some broader issues in compensation than merely matching the going rate.

First, paying higher wages to new employees can be the coup de grace for some established staffers, who now conclude that they've been underpaid and mistreated. To avoid this, some companies raise existing employees' wages at the same time.

The most problematic part of using wages to attract and keep people is that compensation level alone does little to qualify or motivate the right people. Pay is not a long-term motivator. Increases and bonuses may temporarily ignite a person's motivation, but pay level soon becomes an expected feature of the work scene. We will return to this point later when we look at compensation in more detail.

Orientation

The very first day of employment is a crucial one for setting expectations and answering employee questions. New employees bring a natural level of enthusiasm and curiosity with them to a new job. Just as a new-car owner relishes his or her first spin with the new wheels, so do most new employees look forward to the first few days of their new job. No employer should lose this precious opportunity to set expectations and answer questions.

But Ralph Raymond was so anxious to have a new customer service rep that he thought, "I need Warmbody to get right to work. He can find out where the cafeteria is on his own." Ralph overlooked the fact that he is not just a buyer but a seller of employment.

Ralph also sees the situation of hiring a new employee like that of buying a new car. A new car buyer is understandably anxious to try it out as soon as possible. A manager is understandably eager for a new employee to get to work as soon as possible.

Particularly when a position stays open for a long time, a manager may accumulate a backlog of work that a new employee must face. Unlike a new car, however, a new employee is likely to be in a "new buyer" state of mind, the same way the manager is. Managers can unwittingly turn off a new employee's enthusiasm and curiosity by failing to help him or her make a smooth transition and overloading him or her from the first days on the job.

Training

Ralph Raymond's philosophy of training is embodied in the saying, "Smart people learn on the job. That's what we're paying them for, isn't it?"

At Wonderful Widgets, little time is devoted to training. The workload in customer service is staggering, and experienced employees have no time for giving much training to their new co-workers. Training is to occur "as it is needed"—in effect, in between or during phone calls, by more experienced employees. There is little incentive for them to perform the training, though. The implicit message to new people is, "It's part of your job to learn it on your own."

Sometimes people learn what they need to know on the job, and sometimes they don't. The question is whether a company can absorb the mistakes that untrained or informally trained employees will inevitably make.

Management and Leadership

Wonderful Widgets has a management and leadership problem. When Ralph Raymond saw Joe Warmbody failing in his job, he said to himself, "I told him what I wanted done. This guy just can't cut it here. I'm not a mother hen!" Warmbody's response to the failure was to stop trying. Feeling a lack of support, he turned hostile. Unfortunately, even the most highly trained and motivated employees lose effectiveness if they are unmanaged or poorly led.

Ralph Raymond and his type feel that some amount of employee dissatisfaction is inevitable. "People are at work to produce, not to feel good," he says.

A few years ago, a human resources vice president invited the authors to give a sales presentation to the senior executives of a large insurance company. The subject we were to address was employee surveys. Our client wanted to tackle what he saw as a problem of lagging morale.

Just after we were introduced and just before we started our presentation, the company president leaned across the table and expressed an interesting view to us. He said, "Son, I think people are like tissue paper. When they get used up, we throw 'em away and reach into the box for another." He wanted to know why, given his view, he should even consider conducting an employee survey.

There seemed no good response, given his position—except that quality people have many options today and to point out the high but somewhat hidden cost of unmanaged turnover. Paradoxically, many managers now know they *can't* take this approach. Managers like the insurance company president may think they're up-to-date and view themselves as very successful in implementing their management knowledge. But unfortunately for them, those on the receiving end often don't see it the same way. This is well documented by industrial psychologist Clark Wilson, as shown in table 2–2.

The differences between managers' and subordinates' ratings in table 2–2 may seem small. However, they are averages generated by a validated survey instrument on over ten thousand individual cases. Some of the discrepancies are in fact very large, and they show a potential for serious problems.

Table 2–2

Two Perspectives on Performance of Fundamental Management Skills
(Average Rating on a Scale of 1 to 7[a])

Management Skill	Managers' Perspective on Themselves	Subordinates' Perspective on Their Managers
Maintaining a time emphasis	5.3	4.8
Recognizing good performance	5.5	4.7
Technical and functional expertise	5.1	4.7
Clarifying goals and objectives	5.2	4.5
Encouraging participation	5.5	4.5
Facilitating the work of others	5.3	4.4
Providing honest and useful feedback	5.3	4.4
Organization and work planning	4.7	3.9

Source: study of more than 10,000 surveys of manager skills.

Technical Report on Perceptions of Management and Leadership Skills (Silver Spring, Md.: Clark Wilson Publishing, 1990).

[a]*Key*:
1 = Low score (management skill *is not* being performed to any extent)
7 = High score (management skill *is* being performed to a very great extent).

If I, as a manager, think I am doing something very well, I'm not likely to try to improve my skills further. If in fact I am *not* very skilled, and if that is obvious to other people, then I am potentially at a dead-end. Others see that I need improvement, but they aren't telling me where I need it. I therefore don't know where to focus my own improvement efforts, so productivity improvements remain at a standstill.

Wilson's studies have found similar problems among leaders as among managers. Table 2–3 shows the differences in perspectives between fifteen hundred executives and their manager subordinates through a similar validated survey of skills.

Morale

"People are here to produce, not to feel good," says Ralph Raymond. Managers like Ralph don't understand the differences between good morale, positive motivation, and high employee pro-

Table 2–3

Two Perspectives on Performance of Fundamental Leadership Skills

(Average Ratings on a Scale of 1 to 7[a])

Leadership Skill	Executives' Perspective on Themselves	Managers' Perspective on Their Executives
High personal standards	6.0	5.6
High standards of performance	5.6	5.5
Willingness to take risks	5.6	5.2
Sensitivity to organizational issues	5.2	5.2
Perseverance	5.4	5.2
Good ideas and strong business vision	5.3	5.0
Awareness of personal influence	5.1	5.0
Managing personal stress	5.2	5.0
Recognizing contributions of others	5.4	5.0
Persuasiveness	5.1	4.9
Ability to generate teamwork	5.3	4.9
Amount of push or pressure	4.6	4.4

Source: study of fifteen hundred individual executives' leadership practices, *Technical Report* Clark Wilson Publishing.

[a]*Key*:

1 = Low score (leadership skill *is not* being performed to any extent)

7 = High score (leadership skill *is* being performed to a very great extent).

ductivity. Contrary to what some may believe, good morale does not always lead to positive motivation. Positive motivation does not always lead to high productivity. Furthermore, Ralph Raymond doesn't understand that his work team's productivity is directly linked to his management skill.

Good morale in a workforce primarily reflects satisfaction of employees. Positive motivation, an internal state of readiness to act, is different from morale. High productivity is a management outcome, the effective channeling of motivation toward a business objective.

Employees who are highly achievement-oriented feel success in reaching the business objective. To them, this is satisfying, and hence, linked to morale. For employees who are not achievement-oriented, a relaxed work environment may be highly satisfying and achieving the business objective might be quite secondary. The morale of this group might in fact be linked to their level of relaxation or stress.

The bottom line is this: Satisfied employees are not always effective and effective employees are not always satisfied. Morale is thus not a sure road to improved productivity. While positive morale makes management easier, it is not directly linked to effective performance.

In fact, management skill is more strongly related to effective work outcomes than morale. This has been made very clear in work by Dr. Frank Shipper at Arizona State University. Shipper used management and leadership survey instruments from Clark Wilson Publishing to document the differences. Shipper's statistical evidence shows a very clear positive relationship between a manager's mastery of management skills and the effectiveness of his or her work unit.[1]

Says Shipper, "I have found a number of work units with high morale, but average productivity. The key skill which was missing was exercise of control by the manager. The managers were "cheerleaders" and "nice people," but the product or service delivery was only average. He notes that "nice" managers don't harvest effective performance any more readily than "nasty" managers. "Only a minority of the employees in these work units responded to the cheerleading."

Thus, Ralph Raymond has a point when he says, "People are here to produce, not to feel good." What he doesn't grasp is the role he must play in their productivity.

Turnover

"Vote with your feet," is Ralph Raymond's thinking on the subject of turnover. "If you don't like it here, find a new job." He believes turnover is a good way of "weeding out the bad ones."

Think of the same situation in a customer-supplier context. Occasionally, a sales or marketing manager may say, "I'm glad that customer left. He was getting to be a problem." But more commonly, good salespeople try to *keep* good customers. Similarly, competitive employers try to *keep* their best people. They manage their turnover—they don't get managed by it. Unwanted turnover may happen, but competitive employers try to make turnover happen at a time and pace that they themselves choose—not by employees randomly fleeing a negative work environment.

At Wonderful Widgets, "good riddance" is the only sentiment when Joe and other "malcontents" leave.

A lot of bad feelings—and bad public relations—were generated during Joe Warmbody's tenure. Not only was Widgets in the process of losing an unhappy employee, but his message went to a lot of other potential recruits as well.

In combination, the errors made by Wonderful Widgets and Joe Warmbody led to a failed employment partnership. Table 2–4 highlights the most serious mistakes that companies like Wonderful Widgets make in relation to their employees.

Wonderful Widgets as a whole espouses the more benevolent parent-child model of employee relations, but Ralph Raymond still operates in the master-slave frame of mind. He assumes that staffers should accommodate him and his practices. Unfortunately, this leaves Wonderful Widgets in a perpetual state of recruiting, interviewing, hiring, and finally terminating its increasingly expensive hires.

We hope this visit to Wonderful Widgets has made one simple point very clear: A tight labor and skills market demands the elimination of poor employment and management practices. When qualified people feel they have options, they exercise them. If you are not prepared to meet employees on a playing field that is more level than you are accustomed to playing, you are in for a rude surprise.

Noncompetitive employment practices are anachronistic today, when the right people are hard to find and to keep. Today's employers are not only buyers of people's services but also sellers of their companies as good places to work. In the following chapters, we'll explore the five attitudes by which you can meet this double challenge:

1. Be definite
2. Understand the ideal candidate's vision of ideal employment
3. Use candidate-centered communications
4. View selection as a service
5. Be retention-oriented

Table 2–4
The Competitive Impact of Eight Employer Mistakes

Mistake	Impact	Solution
1. Company-centered communications in advertising and other recruiting	Fails to fulfill a potential employee's need for information about the job and the company. May intimidate or offend the potential employee. Is unlikely to elicit as many positive responses as communication designed to speak to the potential employee's interests.	Candidate-centered communication
2. Interviewing based on "gut feelings" alone	Often fails to qualify the candidate appropriately for the job and the company. Can overlook obvious mismatches.	Job-related behavioral interviewing techniques
3. Using compensation to solve "tight labor" problems	Raises costs without improving sales or productivity. Does nothing to qualify the candidate's ability or interest.	Avoid when possible
4. Providing little or no new-employee orientation; failing to focus on the new employee's questions	Interferes with a new employee's desire to enjoy his or her new job. Fails to take advantage of natural enthusiasm and curiosity. Tries to communicate information for which the employee is not ready.	Provide orientation
5. Providing little or no job training	May produce task failures, creating frustration for the new employee. Fails to take advantage of the power of training to satisfy needs for growth and challenge.	Provide appropriate training at the right time
6. Poor management and leadership	Poor management means employees don't know what to do; poor leadership means they don't know why. Leads to low effectiveness. May inspire workers to consider options.	Manager and executive feedback and training

Table 2–4 (Continued)

The Competitive Impact of Eight Employer Mistakes

Mistake	Impact	Solution
7. Tolerating poor morale	Employee has to work harder to obtain what he or she needs from the job. Opens the door to consideration of other options—or simply incents reduced work output.	Survey to monitor morale and address problem areas
8. Unmanaged turnover	Introduces very negative messages into the communications environment, both inside and outside the company. Makes employees think competing companies must be better.	Practice turnover control techniques

Note

1. F. Shipper and C.P. Neck, "Subordinates Observations: Feedback for Management Development," *Human Resources Development Quarterly* (in press) and F. Shipper, "Mastery and Frequency of Managerial Behaviors Relative to Subunit Effectiveness," *Human Relations*, (in press).

3
Be Definite

A sk most managers what they need in order to hire well, and they answer without hesitation: "Good people." Ask them how they define *good people*, and their answers usually focus on the results desired: "Someone who types fast," "Someone who can learn and adjust to lots of different situations," "Someone who really pays attention to detail." The definitions, of course, are as diverse as the jobs and managers themselves.

Ask a professional purchasing manager how to work successfully with crucial suppliers, however, and you'll hear a different story. Successful customer-supplier relationships, they'll tell you, are built on carefully defined purchasing criteria. If you would be a more competitive employer, your first step is to be definite about your target employee.

Unfortunately, these criteria are often missing from the thought process of a hiring manager. People are only as good as their skills, motivation, and "fit" with a situation allow them to be. It is necessary for a hiring manager to profile ideal candidates on all three criteria; otherwise, he or she may be setting up for failure before recruiting has even begun. Indeed, much turnover is designed into employment before a new employee even begins to work. Industrial psychologist Richard Gould offers an excellent example of why it is so important to link business strategy to people management.[1]

Define the Kind of Employee You Need

Consider three retail businesses, invites Gould, each of which has a different business strategy. One is a convenience store, the second is a garden supply center, and the third is a boutique that offers unusual products.

People go to convenience stores because they want to enter, get what they want, and get out fast. The business strategy of a convenience store, then, must meet this customer demand. For the human resources aspect of the convenience store's strategy, it would make sense to find outgoing people who are willing to treat customers in a hurry.

The second retail business, the garden supply center, carries a complete line of garden supply products. Its customers want knowledgeable salespeople who can help them select from among many different but similar products. In this business, the business strategy might be to emphasize certain technical skills when hiring. To accommodate the customer service aspect, employers train employees to provide technical information in easy-to-understand ways.

The third retail business, the boutique, focuses on providing unique products. Customers shop at this store to find things they can't find elsewhere. Yet as the company knows, it isn't easy to get customers to actually try new things. Its business strategy? Let customers try the products, handle them, and hear about the unusual origins of the products. Their sales clerks need to take an interest in the merchandise and develop product knowledge.

Gould's basic point, a good one, is that you must link business strategy to what you need employees to do. You want employee behavior that supports the business strategy. If an employer hires the ideal convenience-store clerk for a boutique, the resulting mismatch is the fault of the employer.

Mary Jones of Wonderful Widgets Corporation recruited Joe Warmbody without giving much time or thought to this first step in her "buying process." True, she had asked the manager what he wanted. True, she had interviewed a number of individuals. True, she had even written a job description.

But none of these steps led to understanding what kind of person would survive the sometimes interpersonally difficult customer service environment. In a nutshell, she had given little thought to what it would take for an employee to "fit" some of the environmental demands of the job.

Now she rightly asks herself, "What good is offering a higher salary if we're simply headed for another Warmbody situation?"

Had Wonderful Widgets managed its recruiting differently, Joe might never have bothered to apply for the job—and Jones might never have hired him in the first place. Jones concludes that Wonderful Widgets needs to "attract to fit."

Recruiting for Fit:
Pepperidge Farm

Corporate Human Resource Manager Patricia Denne says that current employment conditions led Pepperidge Farm to the conclusion that they should "recruit for fit."

"We have a good reputation and we're visible, which aids us in recruiting. But salaries have been driven up by competition," she says. "We made a conscious decision that we wouldn't compete on salaries alone. We felt we could highlight other aspects of the company as well. By promoting those aspects of our company, whether it be benefits or environment, we tap into other values held by applicants."

She says that in the past, Pepperidge Farm recruited for certain hard-to-fill positions more on skill rather than fit. "But the match was obviously not great from the beginning. We had to work very closely with both the employee and the manager to keep it going."

Adds Denne, "Sensitivity to candidate values is important for us. We work with managers to help them see why this is needed in today's recruiting environment. It puts an extra requirement on the manager, who has to make more of an effort to meet people half way."

"The old ways are easier, more black and white. If the employee didn't measure up, you'd terminate. The new environment, where we emphasize development and retention, requires a much more thoughtful and open approach, therefore requiring much more time and energy."

When interviewing, Denne looks for people who want a relationship with their employer. "We have chosen to keep the staff lean at all levels, so we still have a small company environment. We're not overly structured, and there's plenty of opportunity for people to have their say. We look for people who seek these values."

Job Analysis

Job analysis is a technique that builds a bridge between the results the company wants to have and the staff it needs to have deliver them. Long a fundamental activity of companies concerned about fair employment, the power of job analysis as a tool of competitive employment is also great. Job analysis is to competitive recruitment and hiring as market research is to a successful product launch.

Unfortunately, job analysis is not one of the more visible or flashy concepts in management today. To create an analogy, think of job analysis as a way to build a good foundation for a house. Though it is largely invisible and not a major contributor to the aesthetics of the home, its existence is key to the success of the building.

Job analysis can take many different forms. But on a conceptual level it attempts to determine three basic kinds of job requirements:

1. What job skills—performance requirements—must a person bring to the job in order to be successful?

2. What motivational characteristics will the best candidate bring to the job?

3. With what kind of work and people environment will successful candidates fit? By the same token, what kind of environment do they create?

Competitive employers explore answers to all three questions. A highly skilled, highly motivated employee at work in an acceptable job environment is a powerful combination.

Performance Requirements

These are the "can do" demands of a job, the items typically found on job descriptions. They include skills (such as typing and assembling), as well as key knowledge (such as familiarity with accepted bookkeeping procedures). They include abilities gained through education, training, and experience.

For example, if a job calls for keyboard operation, typing at a certain speed and accuracy would be one performance requirement to examine. If the job requires someone to answer telephones, then a clear speaking voice and an ability to communicate clearly may be required.

It is easy to "overload" knowledge and skill requirements—ask for too much—even for entry-level jobs. Doing so makes recruiting and hiring even more difficult because fewer applicants will meet your baseline requirements.

Overloading can also result in unfair treatment of minorities. Interpretation of fair employment legislation has led to the development of a series of both formal and informal guidelines on how to handle knowledge and skill requirements. The net effect is that most employment laws dictate the use of only "bona-fide occupational qualifications" to screen potential employees. This means that you must be able to prove that the requirements that you state are necessary for the job are really necessary.

Equal Employment Opportunity and Fair Employment considerations are reviewed in the appendix. Specific actions and strategies related to fair employment should always be reviewed by your company's legal advisers.

If we were to work on Wonderful Widgets' hiring problem by providing a job analysis for its customer service representatives, table 3–1 shows what we might learn.

Table 3–1
Performance Requirements:
Customer Service Representative

1. Speak simple English, so that both native and nonnative English speakers can easily understand him or her.

2. Write simple customer memos to confirm the content of conversations and/or to request further information.

3. Have basic typing skills (a plus, but not necessary).

4. Have a basic familiarity with the industry—the vocabulary, and a general understanding of how the products are used (a plus but not necessary).

Note: These performance requirements are developed from the checklists at the end of this chapter. See the appendix for rules on "bona-fide occupational requirements."

Motivational and Environmental Requirements

Not everyone who *can* do a job *will* do the job. Less well defined than "can do" performance requirements, motivational and environmental requirements are harder to determine. The opportunities provided by determining them are worth assessing, though, so competitive employers must explore them in their job analysis.

Motivational requirements ask the question, "Will this candidate do this job?" Although motivations are harder to measure than knowledge and skill, managers trained in behavioral or job-related interviewing techniques can become adept at assessing them.

Environmental requirements concern the issue of "fit" between the employee and the company's work environment. This is probably the most difficult employment consideration to measure. How well will a candidate be satisfied in a particular work environment? Again, trained interviewers can become fairly effective at judging a "match." Later we'll describe why it's probably a more efficient strategy to attract the right kinds of applicants (that is, to allow people to "self-select") and to hire mainly on the basis of the other two criteria.

For now, let's examine some of the critical motivational requirements for the customer service representative position at Wonderful Widgets. These are presented in table 3–2.

Now let's look at the critical environmental requirements for Wonderful Widgets CSRs (see table 3–3). Mary Jones correctly observed that skills and motivation are not enough to ensure effec-

Table 3–2
Motivational Requirements:
Customer Service Representative

The customer service representative must:

1. Follow through on tasks without being directed.
2. Persist on a task until a satisfactory outcome is achieved.
3. Be able to understand and state the customer's point of view.
4. Follow rules and procedures, even when it is easier not to do so.

Note: These requirements are taken directly from the Motivational Requirements Checklist shown at the end of this chapter.

Table 3–3
Environmental Requirements:
Customer Service Representative

The customer service representative must:

1. Have frequent contact with people outside the company.
2. Be able to work with people who are sometimes quite tense, even angry.
3. Be able to work in a somewhat noisy environment.
4. Focus on getting a result or resolution to the customer's inquiry. (Often no specified company procedures will directly solve a particular customer problem, so the customer service representative must sometimes figure out how to solve the problem on his or her own.)

Note: This information is the summary result from the Environmental Requirements Checklist at the end of this chapter.

tive job performance. Not everyone who can and will do the job thrives in the employment environment that Wonderful Widgets offers.

Sometimes Mary wishes she could change the employment environment to fit the people who apply for the CSR jobs. "Not a bad idea," says her boss, who then adds, "Maybe our next president will be interested in that."

Jones, always the survivor, takes the hint. For now, she is doing her best to *understand* the actual work environment (which she knows is not completely consistent with the Wonderful Widgets' "Statement of Corporate Values").

Jones focuses on two issues that seem to be common themes in her exit interviews. The first issue concerns the type and frequency of contacts that the employee must make both inside and outside the company. The second issue involves the tangible and intangible aspects of the work pace, the setting, and the expression of company values as they relate to the customer service representative job.

Jones's conclusions for this part of the job analysis are summarized in table 3–3.

Wonderful Widgets now has a simple job profile that addresses three major job-requirement areas. Although all of the considerations could be considered important, Jones knows she has to be practical.

Careful Selection:
Diamond Star Motors

Diamond Star Motors faced the monumental task of hiring twenty-nine hundred people between 1986 and 1989 for a factory startup. A fifty-fifty joint venture of between Mitsubishi and Chrysler, theirs was one of the much-publicized "greenfield" factories that brought Japanese production and management techniques into the United States. Diamond Star determined to build quality into the operation from the beginning. It supported this goal with an extensive program of screening, hiring, and training.

Despite the Japanese reputation for having demanding hiring standards, the Illinois Department of Employment Security received 200,000 inquiries about the twenty-nine hundred jobs at the plant. To manage this phenomenal quantity of inquiries, the consulting firm Towers-Perrin and the joint venture staff executed a rigorous five-step screening and selection process.

The potential applicant took the first step by viewing a "realistic job preview" video. The eighteen-minute video explains the standards, operations, and methods that one can anticipate as an employee. The moderator repeatedly asks, "Is this type of work environment for you?" About 20 percent of the viewers dropped out as a result of the video.

The remaining steps included the General Aptitude Test Battery (GATB), medical tests, drug tests, aptitude tests, questionnaires, individual and group exercises, and of course interviews. "The screening process was so extensive," says Sarah Henry, a Towers-Perrin consultant who managed their assessment center, "that if you reached the fifth stage, there was a 90 percent chance you'd be hired."

The plant's production has reached and exceeded the quality standards set by the Japanese partners.

During follow-up interviews with the new hires, Henry learned why the jobs were so attractive to applicants, who came from places as far away as Hawaii. "People said they were sick of foremen who didn't listen," she says. "They had heard about Japanese management and felt it would be an opportunity to have their involvement taken seriously."

The plant has been in full operation since 1989, although the first people were hired in late 1986. The turnover rate is well below auto-industry standards. "Turnover is in the single digits," says Henry.

If it's not possible to get someone with the required set of skills and abilities through recruitment and hiring, Jones has to consider which of the requirements she can most effectively *train* in a person. If training is impractical or not possible, she can then consider *redesigning the job* to fit either her staffing profile or her training profile. Another approach is to use *technological solutions* that alleviate part or all of a requirement. These alternatives are explored in chapter 10.

Had Jones done this job analysis two years ago, she would have quickly seen in her interview that Joe Warmbody was the wrong person for the job. Although he initially seemed a good match, he was actually different from what Widgets needed in several key areas (see table 3–4).

Mary Jones now has a brief profile of the "ideal candidate," as well as a list of the reasons why Warmbody was never the right person for the CSR job. This "ideal" profile assumes, of course, that there won't be major changes in the work or in the environmental requirements—at least, not changes so large that they can't be handled through redirection and retraining. If such changes do occur, the profile will have to be adapted.

Table 3–4
Wonderful Widgets and Joe Warmbody:
How Good a Match?

What Widgets Needed	What Warmbody Offered
Speak clearly	Good ability
Write simple customer memos	Average ability
Type short memos	Good ability
Follow through without being told	Very good ability
Work until achieving a satisfactory outcome	Very good ability
Understand the customer's point of view	Very good ability
Follow rules and procedures	Very poor ability
Contact people outside the company	Low effectiveness
Work with tense people	Very poor ability
Avoid distractions in a fairly noisy/busy work environment	Very poor ability
Strong "results" orientation	Poor ability

Job Analysis Improves Customer Service

Wells Fargo Bank decided that it would provide its customers with teller service in "five minutes max." The executives realized that this would have a profound impact on their employment strategies, and they used job analysis to develop the link. The result: They now have two job descriptions where there was previously one, which gives them the flexibility to accommodate both career-oriented and job-oriented teller candidates. Best of all, according to Susan Palmer, vice president for human resources, the bank is now serving customers better—who do reach a teller in "five minutes max."

"We created two employment tracks," says Palmer. One, the "Merchant Teller," is designed as a career position. It handles a range of twenty-five banking transactions. The second position is dubbed the "Flex-Schedule Teller." These handle customers who require the four basic, most common transactions. The Flex-Schedule Tellers are "on call" and typically work flexible hours during the peak customer hours in the branch.

Thus, Wells Fargo directs its more extensive training at employees in the career position of Merchant Teller. It offers less training to Flex-Schedule Tellers, but it "markets" the job to people who want part-time and short-term employment. "The expectations are very clear on both sides," says Palmer.

Not only were people employed in ways more closely suited to their goals, but customers were better served.

You can arrive at a similar job analysis by completing the checklists for the position you need to fill (see tables 3–5, 3–6, and 3–7). If you identify too many requirements when you complete the checklists, try to narrow them down. Jobs with many crucial requirements are not only very rare, they are extremely difficult to fill. If you have selected too few requirements and feel that you have missed some important aspect of this position, consider adding the relevant aspect to the checklists. You may want to complete your picture of the job more fully by speaking with job incumbents or managers to identify more key requirements. When finished with your research, use table 3–8 ("Summary Job Profile") to complete the picture.

Table 3–5

Checklist: Performance Requirements

The basic skills required to do a job are an important first consideration. This checklist will help you determine the relevant performance requirements.

The employee must be able to use these basic abilities to perform required job tasks:

[ ] Basic arithmetic (add, subtract)

[ ] Advanced arithmetic (multiply, divide)

[ ] Higher math skills (equations, algebra)

[ ] Basic writing (memos, notes, etc.)

[ ] Business writing (letters, reports, etc.)

[ ] Basic speaking abilities (one-on-one, small groups)

[ ] Advanced speaking abilities (presentations, speeches)

[ ] Evaluating facts and information

[ ] Decision-Making based on facts and information

[ ] Analyzing work problems

[ ] Work planning and scheduling

What other knowledge or skill must the employee possess prior to obtaining employment?

[ ] Specific Job Knowledge (e.g., employment laws, accounting procedures, programming language, etc.). List:

[ ] Specific Job Skills (e.g., typing, operating a computer using a specific application program, etc.) List:

Note: Performance, Motivational and Environmental checklists and corresponding interview questions available through Performance Programs, Box #105, Rowayton, CT 06853.

Table 3–6
Checklist: Motivational Requirements

Review the important motivational requirements for your open position. Check the statements that represent important motivational characteristics that your ideal candidate would bring to the job. Avoid the temptation to require *all* of the characteristics. Managers often overestimate motivational requirements.

The employee is expected to:

[ ] Perform tasks without direct supervision

[ ] Follow through on tasks without being directed

[ ] Search for relevant information without being told

[ ] Overcome unforeseen obstacles

[ ] Develop new methods or procedures when established ones fail

[ ] Follow rules or procedures even when it is easier not to do so

[ ] Suggest new solutions to problems

[ ] Apply a logical approach to problems

[ ] Try new approaches to stubborn problems

[ ] Maintain high performance and high standards, even when tired or bored

[ ] Maintain high standards, even when frustrated

[ ] Establish own "internal" quality standards

[ ] Follow quality standards set by others

[ ] Be able to balance the effects of speed with quality standards

[ ] Work under strict rules or deadlines

[ ] Work under very loose rules or deadlines

[ ] Maintain performance standards under time pressures

[ ] Perform work within strict deadlines

[ ] Work according to strict schedules

[ ] Maintain a good attendance record

[ ] Maintain a good "on-time" record

[ ] Persist on a task until a satisfactory outcome is achieved

[ ] Be motivated to achieve customer satisfaction, whether the customer is internal or external

[ ] Accept new responsibilities

[ ] Adapt to new procedures offered by others

[ ] Adjust to work with very little variety

[ ] Adjust to work with extremely high variety

[ ] Tolerate difficult situations involving co-workers

[ ] Handle difficult situations involving customers and noncompany people

[ ] Work in unpleasant physical surroundings

[ ] Work in physically dangerous surroundings

Table 3–6 (Continued)
Checklist: Motivational Requirements

[   ] Tolerate a fair amount of paper work and administrivia
[   ] Adjust to predictable changes in workload
[   ] Adjust to unpredictable changes in workload
[   ] Adjust to changes in routine
[   ] Adjust to changes in schedule (overtime, shifts, etc.)
[   ] Adjust to changes in pace and pressure
[   ] Adapt to frequent interruptions
[   ] Adjust to a "fast" pace
[   ] Adjust to a "slow" pace
[   ] Adjust to constant changes in direction or "marching orders"
[   ] Work under very tight deadlines
[   ] Work under fairly flexible deadlines
Other Important Motivational Factors (list below):

Table 3–7
Checklist: Environmental Requirements

Check off the top environmental requirements for the job, the statements that represent important factors in the work environment to which a person must be well adapted.

In working and communicating with others, the job holder must be able to:
[   ] Work alone
[   ] Work with others
[   ] Have contact with people outside the company
[   ] Have no outside contact
[   ] Communicate by telephone
[   ] Communicate in an informal setting, one-on-one, or in small groups
[   ] Communicate formally or to large groups
[   ] Work with people who are sometimes quite tense
[   ] Work with the same people every day on the job
[   ] Meet new people every day on the job

Table 3–7 (Continued)
Checklist: Environmental Requirements

[ ] Accept direction as set by others
[ ] Set own direction
[ ] Work with employees from different departments directly
[ ] Achieve compromise with others
[ ] Accept compromise as determined by others
[ ] Participate in a largely informal communications atmosphere with management and co-workers
[ ] Participate in a rather formal communications atmosphere with management and co-workers
[ ] Follow an informal dress code
[ ] Follow a formal dress code

The employee is likely to experience the following in your location's environment.
[ ] Work with many others in a large office/plant location
[ ] Work with a small number of others in a small office/plant
[ ] "Homey," informal setting
[ ] "Corporate," formal or businesslike setting
[ ] Private work area
[ ] Open work area
[ ] Quiet environment
[ ] Noisy environment
[ ] Work in one place
[ ] Work in many places
[ ] Work with people
[ ] Work with things/ideas
[ ] "Early morning" culture
[ ] "Late afternoon" culture
[ ] Work long hours commonly
[ ] Work long hours uncommonly
[ ] "Team" environment
[ ] "Hero" environment
[ ] Results count more than procedures
[ ] Procedures and results both count
[ ] Workers generally are active participants in business decisions
[ ] Management is generally autocratic
[ ] Employees have lots of company support structure behind their jobs
[ ] Employees have to invent and establish their own support structures

Table 3–7 (Continued)
Checklist: Environmental Requirements

The employee is likely to observe the following management values:

[ ] Experimentation is encouraged, even if it results in honest failures at times
[ ] Action is favored over planning and analysis
[ ] Analysis and planning usually precede action
[ ] Career development is unstructured and based purely on results
[ ] Career development is structured and based on seniority, training, experience, and results
[ ] Management is highly visible and interactive
[ ] Management is relatively reserved in employee communications
[ ] Customer satisfaction is a major driver behind management decisions
[ ] There is a dominant function force in the company, such as marketing, sales, engineering, manufacturing, or finance

Management wants or expects employees to:

[ ] Set their own priorities within general guidelines
[ ] Approach work projects in their own way
[ ] Work alone, on their own
[ ] Have a lot of control over many aspects of their work
[ ] Deal with ideas and concepts, not just concrete things
[ ] Work as team members
[ ] Do exactly what they are told needs to be done
[ ] Relax and be a little playful on occasion
[ ] Take a few risks in their work, try some new approaches
[ ] Say exactly what they think
[ ] Be in friendly competition with their co-workers
[ ] Work steadily, whether or not they are not closely supervised

---

Much professional ink has been poured into the subject of matching people to job descriptions. We reference some of the best known and most useful in the bibliography.

More formal methods of job analysis follow the same procedure we have used, but with some additional steps. Instead of relying on a single perspective, the formal methods also involve people who have done the job and first-line management. For example, you might also validate the analysis by comparing performance of

Table 3–8
Summary Job Analysis

Using the lists you just completed, summarize the information from these exercises.

First, list below your "top three" (or however many you need) performance requirements (basic skills required to do the job):

1. _____

2. _____

3. _____

Second, choose the "top three" motivational requirements (regardless of what subcategory they are from):

4. _____

5. _____

6. _____

Finally, choose the "top three" environmental requirements with which this employee will have to be comfortable:

7. _____

8. _____

9. _____

Other factors:

10. _____

11. _____

12. _____

current employees to their capabilities on the identified job requirements. The best employees should have more of these capabilities than those who are less effective.

Validation shows how well your hiring practices help you find the right people. Due to the technical and legal nature of the subject, consider contacting qualified professionals to help you in the design of such a project.

Job analysis, whether practiced formally or informally, can lead you to make better employment decisions. But compete only for employees who are right for your company. The employees you select, although they might be more difficult to find, are those who are most worth your expensive recruiting, training and employment efforts.

In the next chapter, we'll look at what an ideal candidate might be seeking in his or her ideal employer. This is the second part of the strategic approach to competing for employees.

Note

1. Richard Gould, "Implementing Your Strategy for Gaining Competitive Advantage," address at Fairfield University Management Training Institute, April 27, 1989.

4
Know the Candidate's Vision of Employment

I n the last chapter you developed a profile of the right person for the job that is open. You'd ideally like the people who meet that profile to consider themselves as in the market for your job. Now you must help them identify your company as the right one for them.

To do that, you must understand how the ideal candidate sees his or her ideal job. This is the second major step towards more competitive employment.

Marketers focus on the vision of life as the buyer would like it to be. The classic Clairol hair-dye campaign is an excellent illustration.

A simple question fueled the appeal. "Is it true blondes have more fun?" Notice that the phrase says nothing about the hair dye it advertises. It teases the buyers' imagination and makes them wonder, "How do I find out if blondes have more fun?"

Imagine the difference in Clairol's fortunes had it advertised its product features. "This is a hair dye that does its job without making your hair dry or brittle, or turning it green." Clearly, the first appeal is more compelling. The quest for "more fun" is centered on the buyer.

No, you're not selling fun—or any employment feature on which you can't consistently deliver. The Clairol example offers a lesson, however. Successful advertisers enhance their appeals through customer-centered thinking. You can enhance your appeal to the right people with candidate-centered thinking. When marketers plan product offerings, they investigate what the product means to the potential customer—beyond the physical item for sale. You, too, can plan an employment offering that speaks to a bigger picture—the multiple levels of employment needs felt by your candidates.

The Total Employment Purchase

Recall the last time you dined at a restaurant with a top-notch reputation. In the most basic sense, you bought a dinner. But chances are, you measured your satisfaction on a great deal more than the food. Service, presentation, price, atmosphere, the clientele, and your sense of relaxation were all likely part of the evaluation. In fact, you were buying an experience—the food was, in a way, a vehicle for your expectations.

Employment is a vehicle toward a job holder's expectations. Respected employers gain their good reputations for reasons beyond the jobs they offer. Issues of self-image and social image and a wide variety of other nonjob factors enter into the employee's evaluation of an employer.

Figure 4–1, borrowed from the marketing discipline, illustrates the point. It presents a diagram of the "total employment purchase," including both the tangible and the extended features that a candidate seeks in his or her ideal employment situation.

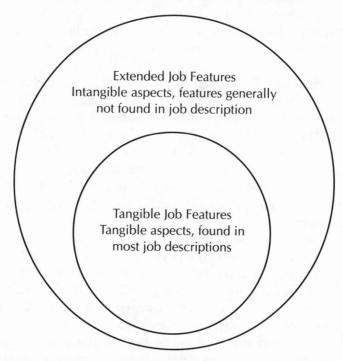

Figure 4–1. *The Total Employment Purchase*

At the most concrete level, the candidate might want a competitive wage and a job that uses his or her skills. At a somewhat less tangible level, the candidate will want to know if the job will have the right amount of challenge, a compatible supervisor, and a quiet work environment. Candidates wonder if they'll be comfortable working in your company. Such questions range from the social ("Is it the kind of place where everybody is expected to join the softball team?") to the ethical ("How would the company react if a product was shown to be unsafe?") to the personal ("How much overtime is really expected?"). These questions are very difficult to ask during interviews, but they are very much present in the mind of a typical candidate (see tables 4–1 and 4–2).

Table 4–1
Total Employment Purchase:
Tangible Job Features

Potential employees may be concerned about:
• Evaluation of compensation and benefits
• The type of work
• Perception of the physical work environment
• Daily work tasks

The following incident illustrates the "total employment purchase" concept very well. Several years ago, one of the authors conducted an employee search for a human resources program coordinator at a nuclear power plant. At the beginning of the interview, all seemed to go very well. The job, the geographical location, the hours, the salary were all on target for the candidates. But after we revealed that our client was the regional utility and that the office location was just inside the fence at the new nuclear power plant, one candidate laughed and said, "Me, work in a nuclear plant? You've got to be kidding." He walked out, saying he was afraid even to drive near a nuclear power plant, let alone work in one.

If Wonderful Widgets had studied the tangible job features as perceived by their target candidates, the company might have developed a list like this:

1. Minimal paper handling
2. Rapid access to people with answers
3. Priority system
4. Comfortable telephone equipment
5. Competitive pay
6. Competitive benefits

Mary Jones might have learned that these extended features are also important to her target candidates:

1. Flexible scheduling

2. Manager experienced or trained in customer service function

3. Support for the customer service function as professionals

4. Quiet environment

5. Opportunity to be promoted within the company

This information provides the basis for powerful communications. It is fairly easy to get, especially if you already employ people who do the work successfully.

Yet much recruiting reflects company-centered thinking. This is unfortunate because an applicant's first meeting with a company is often in such communications, whether in print, through a recruiter, or other means. In truth, company-centered communications can lead to the wrong people applying for your positions.

Open your newspaper to the job ads on any day. A quick look will show you plenty of ads like this one (identifying information has been removed):

> XYZ Ventures, the personal computer industry's premier developer of XYZ software, is seeking qualified individuals for the position of Test Analyst. As a candidate you must have IBM PC or Macintosh experience and demonstrate good communication and organization skills. A BA/BS is desirable. If you think you're the best and are looking for an opportunity with an industry leader, we'd like to hear from you. Please send resume and cover letter to PO Box . . .

Table 4–2

Total Employment Purchase:
Extended Features

Potential employees may be concerned about:

- Overall comfort level with the products
- Overall comfort level with the people
- Overall comfort level with the company's public image
- Overall comfort level with industry's public image
- Perceived fit with personal life and personal priorities
- Attractiveness of the location
- Attractiveness and "comfort" of the current facility
- Availability of public transportation
- Adequacy of area highways at handling peak-hour traffic
- Adequacy of parking
- Availability of affordable housing within the immediate area (five miles)
- Availability of affordable housing within the commuting area
- Attractiveness of available housing within the commuting area
- Cost-of-living expenses within the commuting area
- Perceived quality of immediate management
- Perceived quality of top management
- Perceived potential for job challenge
- Perceived potential for job or career growth
- Perceived potential for recognition
- Perceived level of participation
- Overall level of customer satisfaction
- Market perception of the company's products and services
- Overall market/industry growth
- The company's success relative to the competition
- The company's level of technological sophistication
- The industry's level of technological development
- Untapped opportunities in the industry
- The cyclical nature of the business, creating uncertainty about jobs
- Impact of economic trends on the firm

As an employee, you may think you're the best, but no aspect of this ad is particularly appealing or shows you how the job might be uniquely positioned to suit your career, salary, or location goals. Another glance at the local newspapers also reveals ads like this:

Wanted: Administrative Assistant. Provides administrative, analytical and secretarial support for Chief Financial Officer. Must be PC literate, Lotus preferred. Must possess solid math skills, organization skills and the ability to work under pressure. Dictation skills are a plus. Starting salary: low $20s.

Sound like more fun than a barrel of monkeys? This person must be skilled (PC, Lotus, math), willing and able to do secretarial work (typing and dictation), and able to respond gracefully when the boss says, "Hurry up" (work under pressure). What does this lucky candidate get in return, besides the awesome title of administrative assistant and a starting salary in the negatively worded "low 20s"? We cannot tell from this ad. It's possible that this office is a nice place to work, that the manager is talented, and that the company a successful one. But we'll never know from this ad.

The Role of Candidate Research

A marketing manager would discover customer perceptions by conducting market research, either formally or informally. Product and market research command millions of dollars and hours of effort each year. Marketers justify the expense against the increased earnings they can expect with more perfect market knowledge.

Employers have been slow to transfer this thinking to their human resources efforts. This is particularly unfortunate, since employee and candidate research can be accomplished with comparatively little effort and money. Some research methods include:

Focus Groups

Long a staple of market research, some employers use focus groups to help determine a number of issues. They can function as a precursor to more formal, statistical research. They are very effective in obtaining employee's views on current issues, problems and strengths.

The Need for Eye Appeal

"Manufacturing jobs lost their eye appeal, particularly to young people," says Frank Scalia, corporate director for management planning, staffing, and development at Barnes Group, Inc. "We've concluded that people are staying away from manufacturing in droves because it has a poor image. It starts with our media, and with parents and teachers. We are constantly reading about declining opportunities in manufacturing.

"The market has overreacted to the news about manufacturing," he continues. "It's like people's views of Pittsburgh, Pennsylvania. It's a forty-year-old, outdated picture. Pittsburgh has changed. Manufacturing has changed."

Barnes Group is a midsize manufacturer that's been established in its hometown for 133 years. Its businesses range from old-line mainstays such as metal springs to high-tech aerospace components. Though it has an excellent reputation among its employees and enjoys very low turnover, new recruits are hard to come by.

"The media have told young people to become investment bankers or work in service jobs," he says. "I watch them travel twenty-five miles every day into city traffic jams to do jobs with the insurance companies and other service businesses. I think they ought to know that many jobs are extremely similar, whether you work in manufacturing or service. There is another option right here in their hometown."

Scalia and his human resources counterparts are working with high school teachers to update their impressions of the modern manufacturing environment.

At Barnes' Associated Spring, Human Resources Manager John Fasolo is promoting a cooperative training effort among the State of Connecticut, the local Chamber of Commerce, and the New England Spring Manufacturers Association at area technical schools.

At Barnes' Windsor Manufacturing, Industrial Relations Director Bob Chapman works with local vocational programs to find and encourage students. They provide financial and employment incentives for successful candidates.

Scalia himself is involved with programs that introduce teachers to the realities of modern manufacturing. "After the first session," he says, "I came to realize that teachers had no idea who we are, what we make, or why we're in business. They didn't understand modern manufacturing and had nothing positive to tell students."

Engineer Shortage: Do We Market Ourselves Poorly?

Society of Women Engineers president Maggie Hickel sees a huge opportunity for engineers over the next several decades. Yet fewer students are choosing to major in engineering than ever. "We expect a 25 to 30 percent increase in the number of engineering jobs between now and the year 2000," she says. "Furthermore, the opportunity will always be here. Technology is here to stay. You'll always have a job if you're a good engineer."

One problem, she says, is the image of engineering.

"Engineers are not good at promoting themselves and what they do," says Hickel. "It's also a matter of public exposure. You see *LA Law* on TV, not *LA Engineer*. You tune into *The Cosby Show*, and you see a lawyer and a doctor. Engineering just doesn't get the kind of exposure that some other professions do. Also, there's still a little bit of the 'nerd' stereotype hanging around."

"So, one of the problems in filling these jobs is that we engineers have to let people know what an exciting option our profession can be."

The Society of Women Engineers' goal is to promote engineering to women—and to promote women as engineers. It focuses on employers, parents, counselors, and girls themselves. The society holds an annual convention, produces educational materials for girls, and developmental materials for women who are currently practicing in the profession.

Turnover Surveys

People's reasons for leaving can tell you a lot about why others might not join. Research by one of the authors illustrates the point quite well. Table 4–3 summarizes the top "reasons for leaving" given by 150 workers who voluntarily left their companies.

These data suggest that engineers are more interested in recognition than promotion. Thus, on the retention side, offering engineers above-average salary dollars—instead of more opportunities for personal recognition and bonuses tied to achievements—might be ineffective.

Table 4–3
Top Three Reasons for Leaving a Job

Job Function	#1 Reason	#2 Reason	#3 Reason
Administrative	Challenge	Advancement	Pay
Customer Service	Challenge	Advancement	Pay
Engineering	Recognition	Advancement	Challenge
Financial	Challenge	Advancement	Recognition
Computer/MIS	Challenge	Advancement	Pay
Management	Challenge	Advancement	Pay
Professional	Challenge	Advancement	Recognition
Hourly	Challenge	Advancement	Pay

Source: Based on exit-interview and turnover-survey data from 150 former employees from three different major corporations covering the years 1987–1989. *Technical Report on Causes of Unwanted Turnover* (Norwalk, Conn.: Performance Programs, 1990).

Note that three of the eight groups don't even include pay among their top three reasons for leaving. The key point is simple and often overlooked: Appeals that are meaningful to one group may mean less to another.

Industry and Professional Associations

In many industries, special tasks forces and committees are now investigating how their professions can train, recruit, and hire motivated people. The work done by these groups can provide you with valuable insights at relatively low cost (see "The Need for Eye Appeal" and "Engineer Shortage: Do We Market Ourselves Poorly?").

Professional Recruiters

Ask recruiters for the key points and key hooks. Recruiters make their living by competing for employees (see "Matching 'Ideal' Employers and Employees" and "What Professional Recruiters Wish Their Clients Knew").

Your research may be formal and extensive or it may be informal and intuitive. If your goal is to be more competitive, the key issue is to discover points such as these:

- What are the job, company, and employment features of greatest importance to your best people?

- How well does your company's employment perform against the items of importance?

- What will your best candidate seek in his or her ideal job and company?

- Why do your best people stay with the company?

Just as marketers seek the flexibility of planning total products on multiple dimensions, so you can plan a total employment offering that speaks to multiple levels of job needs felt by your candidates. You may indeed discover an appeal with the awesome simplicity and persuasiveness of Clairol's famous one-liner.

Matching "Ideal" Employers and Employees

Executive recruiter Charles Lubner has conducted searches for fifteen years on behalf of "Big 8" accounting firms. Though his typical recruit earns between $80,000 and $400,000 annually, executives are just as difficult to find and match with his clients' goals as entry-level workers.

"My job as a recruiter is to interview the company and determine the work environment," says Lubner. "I look for company values and use this information to recruit and attract the right candidate. As a recruiter, the most important part of every interview is determining the candidate's point of view on his or her 'ideal' job. It is this one item alone that helps me to determine whether or not there is a match.

"If there is a match," he says, "I start to prepare a list of points that are centered on the candidate's concept. If there is no match, I waste no time."

What Professional Recruiters Wish Their Clients Knew

Recruiters make their living by competing for candidates, and they make their reputations by finding the best ones. Roseanne Shegirian, a ten-year recruiting veteran who runs her own firm, outlines how firms can make the best use of recruiters in a tight labor and skills market.

"A good person was always hard to find," she says. "Now it's extremely difficult because you're dealing with candidates who are oriented toward what you can do for them, not what they can do for your client's company."

Money and benefits are key issues, but they are not the only issues, she says. "More and more, people want to know how they can really expect to be treated by a company." This includes the type of manager they'll have, co-workers, and attitudes of upper management. "People today are particularly interested in knowing whether they'll have any input."

Shegirian also says that the perceived opportunity for promotion is a key factor. "A lot of people feel plateaued," she says. "An opportunity to get off the plateau is very attractive."

She offers examples of two firms who use her services "to greater or lesser degrees of efficiency."

The first company insists that Shegirian and other recruiters work only with the office manager and make no contact with the president. "This greatly prolongs the process," says Shegirian. "It makes it nearly impossible to move quickly."

The second company allows her to make contact with all parties concerned, including the personnel department, the hiring manager, and the company president. "They give me immediate feedback, and they trust my screening evaluation, so we can work with a candidate who hasn't prepared a resumé."

Of the two firms, she says, it's no surprise that the second gets the people it wants much more frequently.

5
Use Market-Driven Recruiting

M arketing technique alone does not a competitive employer make. You may find facing competition easier, however, if you use the tools that marketing has to offer. When marketers plan campaigns, they ask questions like these:

- How many buyers populate the target market?
- Where can the target be reached?
- What appeals will be effective?
- What are their buying alternatives?

Market-driven employee recruiters ask the same basic questions, questions that help them focus on the candidate (see table 5–1). This is the third part of being a more competitive employer.

A local women's clothing shop provides an excellent example of market-driven recruiting. The owner once ran an intriguing advertisement for new employees. It featured her own photo and beckoned readers to "come work with me." The ad described her years of experience as a retailer, the number of people to whom she had taught the retailing business, and her small-shop environment. She relates what led her to this approach.

"I knew from my time as a trainee in a major department store that retailing management personalities can be difficult," she says. "Retailing seems to attract very aggressive people. They can be tough to work for.

"As I got more responsibility along the way, I swore to myself that I would not be the same kind of manager when I owned my own shop. I felt I could handle people better and that this would help me keep them.

Table 5–1
Basic Marketing Concepts as Applied to Employment

Marketing Concept	Employer's View—Related Concept
1. Target market and market segments	Target employee populations target candidate pools—the groups who form your labor supply.
2. Buying decision process	Job Search: From the candidate's or employee's point of view, this is the evaluation and decision regarding his or her employment options.
	Selection: From the employer's point of view, this is the process of finding, evaluating, and deciding on candidates for open positions.
3. "Total product"	Total company and job offering—what employment with your company offers including the job itself, compensation and benefits, company culture, work environment, company reputation, and the other intangibles.
4. Product positioning	Employer positioning—why employment with you is different and better from employment with others, as targeted to the perceived employment needs of selected groups.
5. Communications channels	Methods by which you reach employees and candidates: recruiters, newspaper advertising, word of mouth, employee referrals, internal company newsletters, and any other means of transmitting employment messages.
6. Sales process	Recruiting: Persuading the target pool to contact your company; persuading selected candidates to accept employment.

"Of course, it's been hard to find good store help for several years now," she continues. "To make matters worse, a large shopping mall opened across the street five years ago. I considered closing the shop, but not only because of the new competition. I couldn't get job applicants, and I couldn't afford to simply keep raising the wages.

"Then I remembered what I'd been through as a trainee. I decided to advertise myself as a manager. I felt that I could deliver on the promise of being a low-key, helpful manager."

The first time she used this approach, she succeeded in finding two hires who wanted a career in retailing. Both were still with her two years later. She used the same approach, on another occasion, to attract holiday-season workers. She feels that she attracts people who value the same kind of environment she does—a professional, low-tension environment where cooperation is important. "This is why we're able to continue working together," she says.

Our retailer knew intuitively about the "total employment purchase." She knew from experience what job and company characteristics might represent advantages to her target employees. Without formal planning, she had carried out many of the steps involved with some of the most sophisticated marketing campaigns. She had:

1. Understood that employment is a purchasing process.

2. Defined a target candidate, and determined where she might reach them.

3. Understood needs felt by her target candidate pool, and developed an appeal based on those needs.

4. Positioned employment against her competition.

In short, her actions were centered on the candidate—not on her own company. She used market-driven thinking.

In the following sections, we look at the ways you can apply marketing-communications strategy to your recruiting.

Sizing the Target Market

How many people populate your target pool? How many are likely to want a new job? How many applicants do you need in order to make a good hire? Are some of your target candidates actually current employees of your company already? If you were a marketing manager, you'd ask all these questions about the markets for your product. You'd determine target size through market research, either formally or informally. When finished with your research, the numbers you found could be represented with the information shown in figure 5–1.

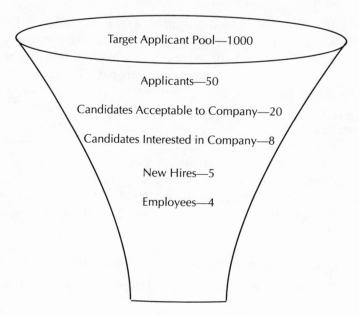

Target Applicant Pool—1000

Applicants—50

Candidates Acceptable to Company—20

Candidates Interested in Company—8

New Hires—5

Employees—4

Figure 5–1. *The Target Applicant Pool*

The goal of the competitive employer is to have enough of the right people enter into the top of the funnel. To do this, the employer needs to know:

1. The size of the target, in its broadest definition, and

2. How the target can be reached most efficiently.

Consider the top of the funnel drawing in figure 5–1 for a minute. This is the largest number of people whom you might consider in the target. Most of them are external to your company, but some may already be employees. You might estimate their locations by following a thought process similar to that shown in table 5–2.

An analysis of the type shown in table 5–2 can help in several ways. First, it helps you prioritize where you'll spend your recruiting efforts. What is the most direct, most accessible, most affordable source of applicants? It makes sense to target these first. A common conclusion would be to target employees who work for your direct competitors and who hold the same job as the one you wish to fill.

Table 5–2
Applicant Locator:
Where Can Applicants Be Found?

Work Experience	Same Company/Same Industry	Different Company/Same Industry	Differ. Company/Different Industry	No Current Job
Same job function	Current job holder	Direct competitors: same job	Company using employees with same skills	Unemployed
Similar job function with similar skill	Employed in related job in company	Direct competitors: related job	Company using employees with related skills	Unemployed
Different job function with transferable skill	Employed in different job but can be trained	Direct competitors: different job but can be trained	Company using employees who can be trained	Unemployed, new-career seekers
No related previous experience	All other current employees and applicants	Competitor employees and applicants	Currently employed workforce	Unemployed, recent graduate

Note: Large, diversified firms may have multiple company units participating in multiple industries. For purposes of this analysis, consider them as different companies in different industries.

Another way this analysis may help is by automatically ruling out certain "markets." For instance, if you are unable to offer any training, you can rule out those with no previous experience, both inside and outside the company. If you do offer training but that training capitalizes on existing job experience in a related job, new work-force entrants and those without related experience will not likely be successful applicants. Such a conclusion, of course, would need to be considered in light of your affirmative action employment plans. Employees holding other jobs in your company (as well as the employees of your competitors who hold related jobs), however, might be a good source of applicants.

A third possible way that using this analysis can help is that it may pinpoint possibilities that aren't immediately obvious. For example, if you need to hire a receptionist, you might be quick to think of recruiting one away from another company in your area; you might even try to recruit one from your direct competitors.

It may be, though, that many receptionist skills are used by people inside your company—such as those in customer service. Is there someone in customer service who would prefer the receptionist job over servicing customer problems? Perhaps you have no internal candidates but there are some at other area companies. How about those who want to be trained for a customer service position? Might they begin as a receptionist?

For Wonderful Widgets' recruiting problem (first described in chapter 2), the "Applicant Locator" grid might look like that shown in table 5–3.

There are potential employees in several of these categories, and those in the same job function in different companies are the most attractive. Mary Jones has labeled those in this category as her "Priority 1" targets.

If Jones is unsuccessful in attracting recruits from her first priority areas, then her second priorities include conducting an

Table 5–3
Wonderful Widgets Applicant Locator

Work Experience	Same Company/Same Industry	Different Company/Same Industry	Different Company/Different Industry	No Current Job
Same job function	Current employees priority: avoid loss	Two area competitors have 15 job holders Priority: 1	Over a dozen companies have 75+ job holders Priority: 1	Job currently in high demand no unemployed Priority: 2
Similar job function with similar skill	Internal 20 potential Priority: 2	Competitors have 100+ Priority: 2	600+? But would require some training Priority: 3	100+? But would require some training Priority: 3
Different job function with transferable skills	50 potential; need for some training Priority: 3	Over 300; need some training Priority: 3	Possibly over 10,000, but need training Priority: 4	400+? But need for training Priority: 4
No related previous experience	Need extensive training Priority: 5	Need extensive training Priority: 5	Need extensive training Priority: 5	Need extensive training Priority: 5

internal transfer and hiring the unemployed. She is reluctant to conduct an internal transfer because she is also experiencing difficulty in recruiting people into jobs from which those transfers are most likely. She also is somewhat reluctant to look at those in the unemployed category since she knows from recent experience that they are very few in number.

If she is unsuccessful in attracting suitable candidates from these categories, Mary Jones plans to target those who would require some job training as her third priority. Those needing somewhat more training but who have some related skills would be her fourth priority. If absolutely necessary, Jones would look last to those who would need extensive training to perform the job.

Jones estimates that the pool for her Priority 1 and 2 target candidates is around 200. If she widens her pool to include Priority 3 candidates, the number increases to more than 1,000. If she is willing to provide more elaborate training and consider those in the Priority 4 category, she estimates her target candidate pool to number around 10,000.

In your own case, you may find more or fewer potential target candidates. The key point is that there are some potential candidates in each category, and that their number depends on both your market and your ability to be flexible.

Reaching the Target Candidates

The local newspapers may reach the homes of your target candidates, but they may also reach several hundred thousand others. This failure of precise targeting is true of most advertising. Since you don't want to waste your valuable resources screening those who don't fit your profile, print ads shouldn't be your automatic or sole choice for delivering your recruitment message.

Many studies have shown that newspaper advertising is the most widely used recruiting method. In recent activity, some employers are availing themselves of other techniques. Some examples:

- An insurance company does a direct-mail promotion to its customers in search of referrals—and encourages customers themselves to apply.

- A marine outfitter advertises for employees in its catalog.

- A group of Chicago employers unites to build and maintain a database of resumés in certain skill areas.

- A major hotel chain uses recruiting handbills at local athletic events.

- A financial services firm uses telecomputer canvassing to generate applications for its sales positions.

- A local tree-service company asks customers to send them names of young people who might enjoy outdoor work during the summer.

To plan a more targeted communications campaign, you need to analyze how your own "group of 1,000" (or 20, or 100, or whatever number) communicates.

The list of recruiting media and methods presented in table 5–4 offers a broad view of the possibilities.

Table 5–4

Recruiting Media and Methods

Internal Resources

[ ] Applicant files
[ ] Internal job posting
[ ] Employee referrals
[ ] Networking
[ ] Customers
[ ] Stockholders
[ ] Suppliers

External Activities and Resources, Nonmedia

[ ] Other firms, seeking to outplace people
[ ] Recruiting agencies
[ ] Executive search
[ ] Public employment agencies
[ ] College recruitment
[ ] Professional associations
[ ] Job fairs
[ ] Open houses
[ ] Minority job-placement agencies

Table 5–4 (Continued)
Recruiting Media and Methods

External Resources, Media-Related

[ ]   Advertising
     Print
     Broadcast
[ ]   Neighborhood establishments
[ ]   Billboards
[ ]   Point-of-purchase displays
[ ]   On-line databases
[ ]   Direct mail
[ ]   Handbills
[ ]   Coupon packs
[ ]   Videotaped ads
[ ]   Publicity
[ ]   Telecanvassing

Communicating with the Target

What appeals will move your target candidate to contact you? The answers are purely subjective—and this is exactly the point of candidate-centered thinking. If you have done your homework and understand your ideal candidate's concept of the ideal employment situation, you have the basis to proceed with marketing communications. This process can unfold in four steps:

1. Segment your employment targets.

2. Compare your company with the candidate's other options.

3. Analyze your company's strengths and weaknesses.

4. Develop "differentiators" and position your employment situation.

Segmentation

When you've identified the broadest possible swath of target applicants, you may benefit from segmenting them. Segmentation won't increase the target's size, but it can increase the leverage of your recruiting communications.

You see market segmentation in action every day. For instance, think about the marketing of a simple product like milk. Many people buy milk, but health- and weight-conscious people, heart patients, and the cholesterol-prone are far more likely to buy low-fat or skim milk. They form a market segment whose requirements are met by a differentiated offering—the low-fat version of milk. With this product, the milk producers keep their customers who cannot or will not buy products with higher fat content. For these consumers, the value of lower fat content is greater than the value of richer-tasting milk.

Segmentation offers you the opportunity to differentiate your offerings. The features that make a difference to one group may have little attraction for another. Your segments may be based on function, geography, factors of fit or motivation, schedule, willingness to train, and many other factors.

Functional Groups. The preferences of an engineer are different from those of a secretary. Secretaries are different from accountants. Technical people are different from art directors. To gain mileage by customizing your appeal, reflect aspects of the "total employment offer" that are meaningful to a subgroup within the target pool. For instance, the fact that your company wins engineering-excellence awards may be less meaningful to secretarial recruits than to engineers and other technical personnel. For secretaries, the availability of training on various computer software may be a plus that would be meaningless to an engineer.

Location. Location is perhaps the classic segmentation factor, dividing those within commuting distance from others. Location continues to be an important factor, but new technologies and work styles have begun to change its meaning.

Geography itself can create a "marketable" strength for a company. For instance, scenic surroundings, excellent commuting conditions, low cost of living, and other place-related factors can be a part of your company's appeal.

Alternatively, the removal of a particular location as a requirement can also form a strength. Solutions such as telecommuting and ex-urban work centers open new geographical areas to the employer. In essence these open new segments to your target pool.

Finding Differences that Make a Difference:
Waldenbooks

At Waldenbooks, one of the nation's top book retailers, Senior Director of Human Resources Maureen Shannon discovered an effective general appeal for MIS (management information systems) candidates through focus-group research. "They're one of the toughest groups to recruit because they're so much in demand," she says. "We know from focus groups that, by and large, people who are attracted to the field are not interested in maintenance—they like to build new, state-of-the-art systems.

"We're very much an information-intensive business, with enormous inventory and order-processing systems requirements. We're addressing our information systems with state-of-the-art approaches. We're also overhauling and automating our work processes.

"We learned in employee focus groups that this actually provides us an edge in recruiting computer professionals—which we've used quite successfully in our recruiting ads."

In the marketing sense, Waldenbooks has discovered that it offers a difference that makes a difference to a hard-to-recruit target.

"Fit" Factors. Perhaps you've noticed this factor at work in the recruiting efforts of nonprofits. These organizations are often driven by a social mission, and they seek people who can consciously support their mission. They are not alone, however.

You may notice employers who advertise for people who are comfortable with a "high energy level," are "able to maintain flexibility," or have "a desire to explore the unknown." These are all ways of describing a work environment that will have appeal to certain segments—and not to others. It is also a way of providing a "realistic job preview" to applicants.

Company culture and management values dominate this type of segmentation. Since such "fit" issues are often at the heart of unwanted turnover, these issues are often critical to your employment success. "Fit" is even more important if your organization is very different from others and therefore very different from what most recruits will expect.

Motivation Factors. Sales managers have long known that money motivation is a plus in candidates for sales positions. From a segmentation standpoint, you might say that the "money motivated" form a segment of the target pool.

Money is a powerful, visible, quantitative marker of success. But other characteristics and motivations also predict sales success. Sufficient interest in customer problems to encourage listening and a sense that the product or service is positively right for a customer are two other strong motivations that are often related to sales success. Our point, though, is that you should use the motivational profile of your most successful employees to help you segment your market.

A motivation toward independence, glamour or visibility can likewise provide a basis for segmentation. All of these states are results that the candidate is motivated to achieve. They are based on the candidate's drive to feel a certain way about himself or herself. Sentences like these characterize such motivations: "I am my own boss." "I am a highly creative person." "I can generate a lot of income through my own efforts." Of course, just saying something like this doesn't make it so. But those who characterize themselves in these terms are far more likely to be the way they describe themselves than are those who don't think of themselves this way. And that is the point of segmentation: it speaks to a specific audience.

Each of these factors provides you with a communications edge because it is candidate-centered. Used honestly, it can help you attract better applicants with your recruiting investment. The picture isn't complete, however, until you understand the target candidate's perceived options.

Competition

The Clairol hair dye campaign was startlingly different, in its day, from its competitors' approaches. It was a competition-beating exercise in creative advertising expression.

Your company's employment competition may be tougher to identify than Clairol's. For example, a client recently asked for a study of turnover among secretaries. He particularly lamented the loss of an excellent administrator who had been with the company less than a year. In an interview, we learned that this administrator had been "pulled" out the door by the promise of promotion out of the secretarial ranks.

She told us, "I know a number of secretaries who got promotions at my new company," she says. "A friend of mine called when a job opened." She had no specific complaints about her previous employer. But her new employer offered something that she desired—a promised opportunity for rapid promotion out of the secretarial ranks. It's key to note that her job move simply held the *promise* of possible promotion, not an actual promotion!

In her view, our client was not competitive in the area of job growth. You need to understand the external factors that attract your employees to other employers. Our client could also have been more competitive *without* offering a promotion to this employee. This would have been possible had they found other differences that make a difference to this employee.

The dress-shop owner at the beginning of the chapter had to combat the benefits packages of larger retailers in her efforts to attract good trainees. She did it by finding strengths that she had and that her competitors didn't—or at least that they weren't creative enough to promote.

Particularly if yours is a small business, you may have a difficult time attracting the right people when you are competing against larger employers. Their competitive advantages may include a nationally known name, as well as (often) better benefits, higher salaries, more glamorous offices, and a variety of other generally favorable points.

The secret to finding and keeping the best people lies in finding a way to position yourself against this competition. The key issue is to identify ways in which you are better and different from them. Being different in and of itself is not important; the differences must be important to your target candidates. Being different in better ways is what makes you a more attractive and competitive employer to them. Finding this out is easier than you might think.

In analysis we offer, you begin by taking a look at your strengths and weaknesses—from the candidate's or employee's point of view.

Strengths and Weaknesses

In the last chapter, the "total employment purchase" questionnaires (tables 4–1 and 4–2) showed the candidate's point of view,
how he or she might evaluate an employer. Hold on to that candidate's point of view for one more step, and you can compare your
company against this list.

Returning to Wonderful Widgets, Mary Jones developed an
analysis of the company's strengths and weaknesses (see table 5–5).
The modern telephone equipment, the competitive salary, and the
extensive benefits that she lists are all desired, positive factors
related to employment at Wonderful Widgets. But are these
desirable factors different from desirable factors of competing
employers?

To answer that question, Jones can analyze an employer to
whom Widgets has lost recruits or employees to determine their
competitive strengths. She gains this information through her
conversations with recruits who choose to work for the com-

Table 5–5

Wonderful Widgets Strengths and Weaknesses

	Strengths	Weaknesses
Desired Tangible Job Factors		
1. Minimal paper handling		
2. Rapid access to people with answers		
3. Effective problem resolution system		
4. Modern telecommunications system	+	
5. Competitive pay	+	
6. Competitive benefits	+	
Extended Work Features		
1. Flexible scheduling		
2. Manager experienced or trained in customer service function		
3. Support for the customer service function as professionals.		–
4. Quiet environment		–
5. Opportunity to get promoted from within company		

petition, and on exit interviews (voluntary terminations only) with employees who have left the company to work for the competition. Her analysis is shown in table 5–6.

The analysis leads you quickly to three important discoveries: There are negative differentiators, positive differentiators, and parity points.

As you can see in table 5–6, an honest evaluation of Wonderful Widgets' strengths shows why the company focuses on pay and benefits as a key attractor for employees. Mary knows she can't compete on the basis of her negative differentiators (such as lack of support and lack of recognition of the customer service function within the company). The playing field is level on the matter of a modern telecommunications system (parity). According to this analysis, Widgets is really competitive on only the two points of pay and benefits.

Jones concludes that a few things must change in order for the hiring and retention situation to improve.

Table 5–6
Wonderful Widget's Competitor's Strengths and Weaknesses

	Strengths	Weaknesses
Desired Tangible Job Factors		
1. Minimal paper handling		
2. Rapid access to people with answers		
3. Effective problem resolution system		
4. Modern telecommunications system	?	
5. Competitive pay	+	
6. Competitive benefits	+	
Extended Work Features		
1. Flexible scheduling		
2. Manager experienced or trained in customer service function		
3. Support for the customer service function as professionals		+
4. Quiet environment		
5. Opportunity to get promoted from within company		+

Differentiation and Positioning

By now, you've identified a target candidate group, understood their priorities, studied the target's perceived alternatives, and pinpointed your own strengths and weaknesses. You are ready to "position" your employment situation.

Some years ago two well-known marketing writers brought out a book called *Positioning: The Battle for Your Mind.*[1] In it, authors Jack Trout and Al Ries explain how advertisers compete for specifically defined pieces of mental turf among their customers and prospects. Positioning, they say, is the process of forming product appeals based on psychological benefits. Positioning aims to communicate the strengths of your offering that are most valued by the target audience—and most favorable in comparison with your competition.

Earlier, we showed how a small retailer battled for the minds of recruits. She "positioned" employment at her store against her employment competitors—other retailers. Where they were strong, she knew she could not tackle them. But where she was strong, she knew she could deliver something they could not.

By positioning your recruiting messages against the candidates' other options, you help them to further qualify their interest. You do this by expressing your positive differentiators.

Positive Differentiators. Positive differentiators are points where your offer is both different from and better than the competition's. For instance, if you offer profit sharing and they do not, you may have a positive differentiator. Notice that we don't say that positive differentiators are absolutely and objectively positive. Rather, they are positive only when they are perceived as such by the target candidate.

Our retailer selected the "tension level in the work environment" as a key candidate concern. She selected "learning opportunities" as another candidate priority. Analyzing her offer on the simple grid shown as figure 5–2, we see that she is positioned into the "positive/positive quadrant" on these two points.

Parity Points. On parity points, you are equal to your competition. You may want to express these to your target candidates along with your positive differentiators.

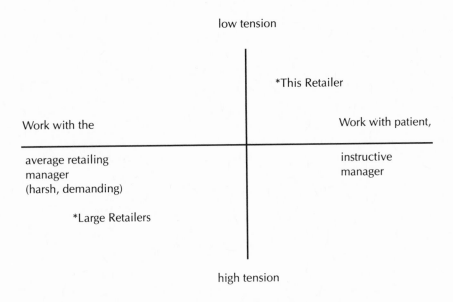

Figure 5–2. *Positioning: Positive Differentiators*

A positioning diagram can help explain parity points. For example, in the case of the dress shop owner who advertised her management skills and attitude as a strength, her statement on a chart would look like that shown in figure 5–3.

Negative Differentiators. Negative differentiators are the opposite of positive differentiators. They are the points where your offer is different but not as strong or desirable as that offered by your competition.

If the point is particularly important in the candidate's eyes, you may need to make changes. Say, for example, that your company offers no health-insurance benefits at all. If other local employers target the same candidate pool as you do, and health insurance is something important to this candidate pool, you may indeed have to change.

On the other hand, if other employers offer a company cafeteria and you don't, you might explain that this reduced overhead allows you to offer a better profit-sharing bonus. Perhaps you don't pay health insurance, but you offer a cash subsidy to em-

Figure 5–3. *Positioning: Parity Points*

ployees. Explain that they can use this subsidy to purchase their own insurance.

It is possible to learn to use your understanding of negative differentiators in a positive way. For example:

1. Target people whose expectations are in line with features that are less than attractive.

2. Build a discussion of these points into your recruiting process so that candidates have realistic expectations about the job.

3. Consider whether you need to improve some of these points in order to compete for the candidates you need. What are the costs and benefits of making changes to attract more candidates? What are the costs and benefits of increasing your recruiting, selection, and management efforts? How do they compare with each other?

On other criteria of importance to candidates, our retailer would not necessarily retain a favorable status. For instance, on

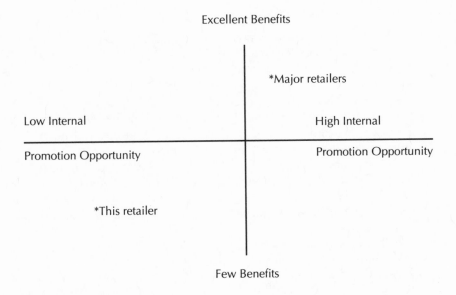

Figure 5–4. *Positioning: Negative Differentiators*

the key issues of benefits and opportunities for internal promotions, she would be less well "positioned" against retailing giants, as figure 5–4 shows.

These simple figures illustrate your position in relation to other employers. They can help you to pinpoint differences that make a difference to your target employees.

Market-Driven Recruiting

The owner of a small retail shop emulated a sophisticated marketing technique when she paid attention to her intuitions about her target candidates' job needs. Whether she knew it or not, she used market-driven recruiting concepts.

Marketers successfully create excitement—and sales—through positive product differentiation that is targeted to the perceived needs of a target pool. Successful differentiation relies on understanding the competition. Even the smallest organization can assess its strengths and communicate them to the people it most wants to

---

The Importance of Expectations:
The Sun Sets on the Night Shift

People have been flocking away from positions that they see as inconvenient, unpleasant, and disruptive of family life. Now these positions, which are critical to manufacturing, utility, and many other around-the-clock industries, go begging.

"Night shifts are particularly unpopular with the younger crowd," one utility company employment manager told us. "Psychologists are researching ways to make these shifts less stressful and make them run better, but in the meantime they are difficult to staff."

This employment manager has addressed the problem by looking for people who have realistic expectations. "We recruit from a plant operators' training program in Bismarck, North Dakota. These people understand the importance of a round-the-clock staffing. To them, its a part of their profession. They are much easier to retain."

---

reach. This increased focus helps advance the cause of finding and keeping the right people.

The steps include:

1. Understand the buying process. Candidates and employees undergo a psychological process that is very similar to that used to make a purchase.

2. Define your target candidate pool in practical terms. How many people are there? Where and how can they be reached? Choose your communications based on the answers to these questions.

3. Research the target candidate's concept of the ideal company and job. Remember that this concept includes both tangible job features and extended features relating to the company, the industry, and other nonjob factors.

4. Position yourself against the competition. Do this with four steps:

a. Identify and study your employment competition.

b. Compare your offers and those of your competition with the candidates' concept of the ideal company.

c. Find your positive differentiators and parity points. Use these to structure your recruiting communications so that candidates understand how your company and its jobs are different and better from their other options.

d. Use your understanding of negative differentiators in a positive way.

  1. Target people whose expectations are in line with features that are less than attractive.

  2. Build a discussion of these points into your recruiting process so that candidates have a realistic job preview.

  3. Consider if you need to improve some of these points in order to compete.

The search for employees has many similarities to the search for customers. Your own candidate searches can benefit from a study of the target pool size and the communications channels that reach it. Help the right person identify yours as the right company. Study your ideal candidate's perceived needs. What does your ideal candidate want from the ideal employer? In what language does this candidate describe the ideal job and company? To make this analysis complete and therefore effective, it must go beyond the simplest candidate requirements such as a "good salary" or "a great insurance plan." It must extend to the work rewards that ideal candidates most value and the type of environment in which they feel most productive.

Note

1. Al Ries and Jack Trout, *Positioning: The Battle for Your Mind* (New York: McGraw-Hill, 1981).

6
Sell Selectively

Competitive employers know that the selection process has two aspects. It allows the company to screen candidates, and it also helps candidates screen companies. This chapter looks at the company's role in both aspects of the process. This is the fourth step in becoming a more competitive employer.

When you are hiring, you are both a customer and a supplier, a buyer and a seller. In your role as a customer, screening and interviewing give you a chance to "shop." This process is your opportunity to come as close as possible to finding the ideal profile built through job analysis.

In your role as a supplier, however, you're called upon to sell your company to the candidates. In this regard, the selection process is actually a service to the candidates. You provide candidates with enough information that they can make an informed decision about a significant business relationship.

There are two basic guidelines for carrying out the "selective sales" approach to hiring:

- Rely on your definition of the ideal candidate to implement your selection techniques, whether those techniques be interviewing, testing, simulation, or some combination of these approaches.

- Rely on your knowledge of that target candidate's concept of ideal employment to carry out your presentation, negotiation and realistic job preview.

First, let's look at screening and interviewing, then at some "sales" techniques that will help you build the right relationship from the beginning.

Screening and Selecting

When the right people are hard to find and keep, it's tempting to "take a chance," to settle for the applicants who are available. This is risky, however, for reasons discussed earlier.

Competitive employers, by contrast, screen very carefully before selling an applicant on employment. They are rightfully reluctant to rely on any one selection method or approach. many prefer to use several methods and then examine a candidate's total profile. Each of the various selection methods has advantages and disadvantages.

Below is a list of the most commonly used selection methods. Some are very simple, while others more complex. Your choice of which to use will depend on a variety of considerations, including their legal implications and their potential effectiveness.

Self-Screening

Since job applicants are actively "shopping" for the right employer, it is natural to give them sufficiently detailed information about the job opening and your company that will help them determine if they would feel comfortable as an employee. It's best for both parties if they walk away, having realized that your company or your job is not right for them.

Self-screening is certainly one of the lowest-cost methods of ensuring that only the right applicants become candidates. Earlier, we discussed the screening methods of Diamond Star Motors. Diamond Star made a video presentation showing the typical work of their employees—as a part of their screening process. This "realistic job preview" video caused an estimated 20 percent of their original applicants to decide that Diamond Star was not the place for them. It was successful in establishing a difference between Diamond Star's expectations and those of 20 percent of their applicants. This simple step saved many of the costs associated with later steps in the screening process, as well as the even higher costs of selection mistakes.

Keep in mind, though, that this procedure—like all other hiring steps—must follow established legal guidelines. It would probably be a bad idea, for example, to use this method for only certain types of applicants (such as walk-ins), or to highlight factors that are not supported by a job analysis. A realistic job preview should be realistic, but it cannot be used as a way to discourage members of protected classes from applying for job openings.

Trial Periods

Trial or probationary periods have been used for many years as part of the screening process, but they may have a new rationale in the current hiring environment. They permit both parties to experience actual employment before they make a more serious commitment.

Trial periods can be costly, however. They often require some commitment to training on the part of the employer. And they always have the potential for opportunity cost. If the trial period fails, you have not only lost your salary and training investment, you have also lost potential productivity. And you need to screen, hire, and train again.

Trial employment periods can present unique legal situations. Like all the other procedures, you must be able to demonstrate the job-relatedness of your decision at the end of the trial period. It is best to treat any "trial employee" the same way you treat other employees—including documenting any failures to perform your work acceptably—so that you will be able to support your hiring decision at the end of the trial period.

Testing

Many employers use testing to predict a variety of factors and to supplement their interviewing skills. The attraction of testing is clear. What employer doesn't want to assess applicant abilities in a consistent, objective way? Give the test, have it scored, and pick the top scorer. What could be simpler?

But testing presents a few drawbacks. First, it is technically difficult to design an accurate, objective test that will actually predict job performance. It requires careful job analysis, development of test items, actual validation (comparison to actual work performance), and a study of adverse impact. This work requires expertise in experimental design, statistics, and test-item development. And, if the job for which the test was developed changes substantially (such as with the introduction of new equipment), the entire procedure has to be re-examined and revalidated.

There is an irony in testing. Well-designed tests, which un-doubtedly predict job performance better than other approaches, must meet a standard that is much higher than other screening measures must meet. Other screening approaches can be defended more easily because they can't be proven or disproved. It is as easy and reasonable to disagree with more subjective approaches, such as interviewing, as it is to advocate for them.

But tests require you to come out into the sunlight, exposing the effectiveness of your procedures to questions and sometimes opening them to intense legal scrutiny. It should be no surprise that there are strict procedures that need to be followed when designing and validating any employment tests.[1]

There are two basic types of employment tests: skill tests and psychological tests.

Skill Tests. Skill tests aim to predict the level of performance of specific job tasks. The best skill tests are carefully chosen for a specific job, and they focus on a handful of specific abilities or characteristics.

All the tested skills and abilities must be supported by a careful job analysis. Tests with the best track record in skill tests are per-formance-oriented (such as typing, climbing a ladder, solving an equation) or situational (such as handling an angry customer, plan-ning a sales call, providing management direction). Well-designed skill tests can provide a better picture of a job candidate's skills than an employment interview alone.

Psychological Tests. Psychological tests, as used for employment purposes, aim to show relationships between psychological factors and actual job performance. They assess a candidate's personal attributes, such as cooperativeness and honesty. Psychological tests have legitimate uses in hiring, but only in specific situations.

The attractiveness of psychological tests in hiring is easy to understand. Most managers are well aware that skill shortfalls are less frequently a problem than are motivational problems. When skill shortfalls present themselves, they are also often relatively easy to fix. The employee can be sent to training or can be coached by more senior employees and management.

But motivational problems are much more difficult to resolve than skill shortfalls. The first step is to identify when you have one, but it is not always easy to distinguish 80 percent performance from 100 percent performance. When you do have a motivational problem, it is often difficult to determine what to do about it. For a variety of reasons, most managers simply prefer to *avoid* motivational problems, and so they try their best not to hire people who are likely to have such problems in the first place.

Psychological testing is one obvious way to try to avoid motivational problems. Because of their careful construction and objective scoring, they have a higher likelihood of measuring psychological characteristics than other approaches have, such as the interview. But there are several problems with using psychological tests. Those problems relate more to *how* employers use the test results than to the tests themselves.

As with other test results, people tend to rely heavily on a numerical score once it has been calculated. Unlike results from other types of tests, though, psychological characteristics tend to be hidden from view by numerical scores. For a "basic arithmetic" test, for example, managers are likely to overlook a borderline test score if the new employee appears to do well when on the job. It is likely they will think that, for some reason, the test didn't work.

Those same managers may even overlook a borderline score on a "work persistence" test if the new employee appears to do well on the job. But many will continue to "watch" for the hidden characteristic, and some will watch for as long as it takes before they observe it. It is easy to be tricked into finding something that isn't really there.

Another limitation is related to the technical difficulty of measuring subtle and complex characteristics. There is always a certain degree of error associated with any test score. These are expressed in their levels of reliability and validity, which you must examine before determining the *range* of scores that are acceptable to you.

The range of acceptable scores is wide for most psychological tests. You can't rely very heavily on the score from a psychological test because if you were to test again or use a different test developed to measure the same characteristic, you would be very likely to get a very different score.

A further problem is that it is hard to demonstrate the job-relatedness of psychological tests, harder than it is for skill or performance tests. It is not always clear how psychological characteristics and attributes actually reveal themselves.

Good Test, Bad Test?

How do you tell a "good test" from a "bad test"? The answer depends largely on what you want the test to do. In the simplest sense, a "good test" is one that does a good job at measuring something you are interested in measuring.

There are two technical considerations in deciding whether a test does a good measurement job. The first consideration is the test's reliability as a performance predictor, also called its consistency. If you administer a typing test to a group of candidates on Monday, and then administer the same (or equivalent) version on Friday to the same group, do the individuals in the group perform at the same level? If candidates haven't brushed up their skills over those few days, any difference you find is the result of an inconsistency in the test.

Reputable test designers always report the level of consistency in their tests. There is no "magic number" to watch for here, though, since there are several different methods of determining consistency. A reliability of .60, for example, indicates that 60 percent of the variance in a score is due to a true difference and 40 percent is due to inconsistency in the test. A "bad test" is one with more inconsistency than you can tolerate. (Interested readers should refer especially to the "error of measurement" section in any good statistics text.)

The second major consideration to weigh in determining a "good test" from a "bad test" is its validity. There are several ways to measure validity. In the job setting, validity usually means how well the test actually measures what it intends to measure.

Employers use validation studies to prove test validity. A typical validation study asks current job holders to take a test. The actual performance and production ratings for this group are gathered. The relationship between their test scores and these actual performance measures provides a validity coefficient. (Interested readers should refer to the discussion of the "error of estimate" in any good statistics text for more information on this concept.)

Validation can be expensive. One recent study found that validation studies cost from a low of $2,500 to a high of $1,245,000 per job—with the average cost around $150,000.[2]

Test developers have been working very hard to answer the sorts of objections to tests discussed above. Many experts believe that because of long experience with basic job skills tests, we can often rely on previously determined validity studies. They claim that for very similar tests being used in very similar situations, employers can rely on "validity generalization."[3]

Validity generalization says that if a test has been proven sufficiently valid in companies A, B, and C, then its validity in company D is automatically accepted. All that is required is to demonstrate that company D is similar to companies A, B, and C. This saves companies the effort of validating an employment study themselves.

Validity generalization is currently a controversial approach, however, with about as many as proponents as critics among industrial psychologists. It involves a systematic analysis of many (sometimes literally hundreds) previously conducted validation studies. Assuming a favorable outcome from the analysis, proponents of the approach claim that the validity of a test "generalizes" to other similar situations. Opponents, however, claim that no two situations are sufficiently similar to provide fair comparison.

Watch out for tests whose validation sample consists of any "highly available" population, such as college students, high school students, or prison inmates. Unless a test was validated against a population similar to that from which you select your employees, you should be wary.

Testing can be an excellent addition to your screening methods. You must be prepared, however, to do it correctly.

While many employers would like to use psychological tests, few actually do as a result of these kinds of limitations. There are some exceptions, of course. You may sleep more soundly tonight after you find out, for example, that nuclear reactor operators and other personnel with "unescorted access" in a nuclear facility must meet certain psychological standards.

Assessment Centers

This screening method asks the applicant to undergo a structured series of exercises and tests, often over several days. These exercises and tests are designed to profile a wide variety of capabilities. They take place at "centers" that are generally staffed by qualified personnel and that are run to fulfill certain specific objectives.

Assessment centers are often used to place current employees rather than select new ones. Many companies use them, for example, to identify early management or executive potential among a group of selected employees. Those so identified are then given increased opportunities to develop the skills needed for future career steps.

The expense of a complete assessment center process, which for management candidates can take up to one full week, is probably the major objection to their use in pre-employment screening. Nevertheless, such screening can help you avoid expensive hiring mistakes.

Employment Simulation

In some ways, simulation exercises are similar to exercises done in assessment centers. Participants in both are carefully observed for how they solve work situations. Trained assessors observe and score each participant based on how they act in each situation.

Simulations can capture some of the best aspects of interviewing and testing. They can also neutralize a person's lack of specific job knowledge. Like interviews, they are done "live." Like tests, they can be scored. They have "right" and "wrong" answers, as determined through a job analysis.

Let's consider a common situation that you, a manager in the process of hiring, are in now. You would like to employ people who have both technical skills and an ability to interact with customers and solve customer problems. But based on your hiring track record, you are unsure of your ability to interview for these required skills. Still, you are unwilling to hire anyone without a defined level of ability.

A job simulation would be ideal. You conduct a job analysis to identify a series of common customer-problem situations. You have your customer service group indicate how well they think that each of several possible approaches to solving the customer problem would work. And you ask all customer service representatives to participate in the simulation, scoring their performance, and comparing those scores both to performance appraisal ratings and to a customer satisfaction survey. You use this information to determine the validity of the simulation.

Because the simulation requires no special product or company knowledge, all candidates have an equal advantage. You can observe and score how well they handle actual situations instead of relying solely on their interview answers and possibly on your own "gut feeling" of how they will ultimately perform. Simulations are an excellent way to understand how a person will act in real work situations, especially those that are difficult to measure or otherwise predict. Of course, like all such selection procedures, the simulated situations themselves must be related to the job requirements, and the scoring procedures must be carefully designed, validated, and implemented. As with the other procedures, only you will be able to determine if your employment needs justify the expense involved in developing a simulation.

Interviewing

The granddaddy of employee selection is, of course, the interview. It is the most flexible and probably most broadly useful technique. A well-structured interview can provide excellent results. Assuming you've found the right quantity and quality of applicants, its potential is limited only by the skill of the interviewer. Unfortunately, interviewing skill is often taken for granted.

The effectiveness of interviewing has always been measured by the interviewer's ability to screen for people who turn out to be successful in the job for which they are hired. There are many excellent books and courses on interviewing as a screening method. Several are listed in the bibliography at the end of this book.

Almost all of these, however, take the "employer-as-shopper" point of view. They teach you to screen and select. There is far less emphasis on your potential role as an employment *salesperson*. In fact, most books on interviewing talk about "the company salesman" as a type of interviewing style to avoid.

A well-conducted employment interview begins like a sales call. The customer is qualified before active selling begins. In this quali-

Table 6–1
Comparison of Steps in the Selling and Hiring Processes

Selling Step	Hiring Step
1. Qualifying the customer	1. Screening: Discovering whether the candidate's skills, abilities, other basic job "qualifiers" match those that the company needs.
2. Probing for needs	2. Interviewing the candidate for motivations, work rewards, and values that determine "fit."
3. Persuasion	3. Presenting the job and company—particularly those strengths that match the candidate's needs expressed in the previous step. Presenting negatives and detractors, perhaps to further the test candidate's interest.
4. Answering sales objections	4. Answering the candidate's concerns about the job, company, or other factors. May require changing some aspect of the final employment offer, such as salary, location, title, or training to be provided.
5. Closing the sale	5. Gaining acceptance of the job offer from the candidate.

fying process, a good interviewer will explore applicants' technical or functional abilities (the "can do"), their work motivation ("will do"), and their environmental needs ("fit").

Numerous sales training programs explain that the selling process unfolds in more or less the same progression of steps as a well-conducted employment interview. Table 6–1 shows these steps and their employment parallels.

To interview well under these circumstances, you must develop *both* a screening method and a sales approach. The following sections look at both sides.

The Interview as a Screening Method

Some managers believe they can hire successfully on their "gut feelings." But as we pointed out earlier, interviewing research tells the opposite story.

To be sure, intuition does play a role in interviewing. The key point to note, however, is that *skilled interviewers use their "gut feelings" or intuitions to guide their questioning, while less-skilled interviewers use their intuitions to draw conclusions.* Skilled interviewers like the interview because it is flexible and powerful, but these are the very features that make it hazardous in the hands of the untrained. Doing a good interview is hard work.

There are two points you need to *know* and one thing you need to *do* in order to screen well during interviews. The two things you need to *know* are:

1. What is the employee going to be asked to do?

2. What behaviors, attitudes, and aptitudes, exactly, are you looking for as indicators that the candidate will fit your needs? What should you find out about each candidate in order to make the right match?

The information you need to accomplish these two goals should be revealed through your job analysis. But without the third step, this key information won't have impact:

3. You need to ask enough of the right questions, while critically listening for the kind of answers that match your needs.

One reason the employment interview is so popular is because it is so flexible. Unlike a test, when an answer given in an interview is unclear or too vague, you get a second chance to find out what the candidate means. Unlike a simulation, in an interview you rely on real past accomplishments in real work settings, instead of relying on artificial (and usually less complicated) situations created for selection purposes.

Interview Based on Job Analysis

Back in chapter 3, Mary Jones used a simple job analysis to determine the job requirements for Joe Warmbody's CSR replacement. Now Jones returns to her job analysis to prepare some interview questions that are targeted to the most important performance, motivation or environment factors.[4]

Performance Requirements: Sample Interview Questions

One of the performance requirements from her job analysis is the ability to write simple customer memos to confirm the content of conversations and/or to request further information.

During her interviews, Jones has two potential sources of information to determine each applicant's abilities in this area: observation and questioning. She can observe:

> How well organized is the applicant's resumé or application form? How well written is the introductory letter?

She knows that these sources of information are limited, though, since many applicants have help in preparing resumés and cover letters. So Jones also asks:

> "Did any of your previous jobs involve writing memos, messages, or letters to customers? Which of these ways do you think is best?"

> "In your current position, how do you go about communicating with customers?"

> "Sometimes people misinterpret what we say or write. Have you ever had this problem? What caused the misunderstanding? What did you do to resolve it?"

Jones would be impressed by an applicant who can describe situations in which he or she successfully communicated via memos or short letters. Responding to the question on misinterpretation, a strong candidate would probably describe a situation in which such a misunderstanding was noticed quickly and he or she took quick and effective steps to resolve the misunderstanding.

Motivational Requirements: Sample Interview Questions

On the CSR job analysis, the position's motivational requirements included persistence. Once again, Jones has the opportunity to ask herself,

> "Was the application form complete? Did the applicant make every effort to answer interview questions completely?"

During the interview, she has several possible questions that she can ask along these same lines:

> "Who was responsible for assuring quality work in your last job?"

> "Were there aspects to your previous job where you really had to work on your own?"

> "In your last job, how did you determine when your work was finished?"

> "What sorts of quality standards were you required to follow in your last job? Describe a situation where you were successful in meeting them. Describe a situation where you were *not* successful in meeting them. What happened?"

The answers the candidate gives will help show how the person self-determines satisfactory from unsatisfactory work performance. The customer service job is one where employees are *not* supervised closely. Therefore, applicants should be able and willing to apply their own judgment of quality to the work product.

Environmental Requirements: Sample Interview Questions

Several environmental requirements emerged from the job analysis as well. One of them was the ability to work sometimes with tense people in a sometimes noisy environment.

Jones lists several possible questions related to this job requirement:

> "Describe a situation where you had a strong disagreement with someone. How did the disagreement come about? How was it resolved?"

"Describe a situation where you were asked to resolve a dispute between two people. How did you go about it?"

"In your previous work experience, have you ever had to deal with a customer, co-worker, or supplier who was upset or tense? Describe what happened. How was the situation resolved?"

These questions will help Jones understand how each applicant handles tense work situations. At a minimum, Jones wants to be sure that the employee will not get disturbed or "frazzled" in such situations. A person who is able to remain composed is unlikely to make concessions, admissions, or agreements simply to reduce the tension.

The Role of Sales Skill

Once you are reasonably certain of an applicant's ability and willingness to do the job, it's time to assume the role of employment salesperson. This may sound obvious, but it may be difficult to implement. The key thing to remember is that the interview should have provided the information you need to present a persuasive case to the candidate. Some information you probably now have:

1. *The candidate's view of his or her ideal "total" employment situation.* If you carried out a thorough interview, you discussed issues of motivation and environment as well as skills. This information now provides you with a picture of the consistencies between the candidate's goals and your own situation.

2. *The discrepancies between the candidate's goals and the situation you offer* are as important as the points where you are consistent. They form the basis for objections, negotiations, and expectations.

3. *The candidate's options.* Many interviewers ask directly, "What other situations are you considering?" You may or

may not get a straight answer if you ask directly; the answer may also come out in questions about the candidate's ideal situation. In either event, you should always ask: "What appeals to you about those situations?" This provides insight into the candidate's perception of your relative strengths.

The point of garnering this information is *not* to equip yourself with ammunition for a high-pressure sales campaign. Instead, the information should provide a basis for an adult-to-adult negotiation and agreement, the classic "win-win" of negotiation.

When people are "shopping for jobs," many of the same psychological processes are present as when they're making a major purchase. They include the following:

1. *Pressure to decide.* Buying is an uncomfortable situation. As long as it goes on, a need remains unfulfilled. The needs of both buyer and seller drive them toward a resolution. To buy, or not to buy. . . .

2. *Self-centered thinking.* This is a time of comparison, when both parties examine how well their own criteria are met. Each is likely to be focused on their own agendas.

3. *A low (or neutral) level of trust.* You want a good employee, and the applicant wants a good job. You may both be motivated to overlook "minor differences." Just as buyers are often concerned that their salesperson isn't telling them the whole story, a job applicant may feel the same way about you. You might also feel as an interviewer that you aren't getting the complete story from an applicant. If the applicant is this good, you may wonder, why did the other employer let them leave?

Therefore, candidates may be very aware of—and even worried about—too much hype. For this and other reasons, your insights on the candidate's thoughts should be used with care. In fact, one of its best uses is the realistic job preview.

Setting Realistic Expectations

In the last chapter we analyzed company strengths and weaknesses. This helped you build positive positioning statements to assist the recruiting process. Along with the strengths, however, your analysis may have identified some weaknesses.

A realistic job preview will introduce your candidate to these weaknesses. This is important because if you proceed past this point and hire this person *without* doing so, you are setting yourself up for a clash of expectations—a clash in which you will probably lose.

So it's not a question of *whether* you present the company's weaknesses, but *how*. For instance, you might try this: "Based on our discussion so far, I'd like to spend a few minutes now telling you more about what our company is like, and what our expectations are of all of our employees. While I think this is a terrific place to work, like anything else, it's not for everybody.

"First, let me describe some of the things that I think people who work here like the most. Then I'll also tell you about a few things some might consider drawbacks."

First, discuss strengths and advantages. Here are some key points to consider:

1. Don't include in your discussion anything that is not—or might not—be true. This strategy is sure to backfire at your expense.

2. Focus especially and carefully on the strengths that make your situation different and better—your positive differentiators.

3. Select and discuss three or four of the positive differentiators that, based on your discussion with this particular candidate, are likely to be the strongest attractors. If you have been unable to determine what these most likely are, you can state the employment features that your previous work has shown are most attractive to other employees. Ask the candidate what he or she thinks or feels about those features. "Is that something that is important to you as well?"

4. Although discussing negatives might seem counterintuitive, research on the best approach for handling weaknesses shows that

being honest about them results in minimal candidate turndowns and greatly reduced instances of immediate turnover.

Introduce the potential drawbacks by indicating that these are some of the reasons former employees have given for leaving your company. Your purpose in discussing them now is to make sure that there really is a match.

For example, you could explain that you have discovered through turnover surveys that a sizable number of former employees found the degree of self-sufficiency expected of them to be a problem.

You might introduce this potential difficulty like so: "In the past, a few employees have had some difficulty adjusting to our management style. We encourage people to be self-sufficient, to try something they think will work well first, before asking for help. In the long run, we have found that our approach encourages creativity.

"Some people are uncomfortable, though, without clearer management direction. One employee who recently left told me he had mixed feelings about our approach. He wanted more direction on how to get things done. I'm afraid that just isn't our style, so we both agreed that he should leave."

You could follow this story up with some additional questions, such as: "What do you think about our management approach? Would you be comfortable working under such conditions? Have you worked under these sorts of conditions before? How did you like it?"

Handling Objections

A realistic job preview is designed to elicit the candidate's objections. If you do it well, you'll succeed in finding and discussing the most important topics. You'll often find these topics posed, however, in the form of objections.

Salespeople are accustomed to hearing sales objections. You should be prepared for several types:

1. *"Drop dead" objections.* These are serious objections that generally can't be overcome. An example might be a secretary, fresh out of school, who demands a starting salary in the "low to mid-60's." Unless your company is accustomed to paying this to

secretaries, the gap between your budget and her expectations is probably too large.

2. *Smokescreen objections*. These are generally reasonable objections that someone uses because they are more appropriate or "nicer" than their more fundamental, real objection.

A classic candidate smokescreen: "Well, that's certainly an attractive offer. I'd like to think about if for a while and get back to you. Maybe I can call you in a few days and we can discuss it some more." While it is possible that your candidate really does want some time to think, the way the objection is phrased hardly indicates enthusiasm or excitement. Most likely, the candidate has some other objection—and that other objection is what you need to discover. It's possible your candidate already has a more attractive offer, or perhaps she is reasonably certain that she will get a better offer if she is patient.

You might respond to such a smokescreen by saying: "Well, just so I can be ready to discuss this with you again, can you tell me what are some of the most important issues you'd like to discuss?" Usually this sort of question will uncover a real objection, such as "I'm not sure I have the skills I need to actually do this job," or perhaps "I need to check out the commuting situation before I decide." Once the real objections are out in the open, you can try to answer them effectively. Don't passively accept smokescreen answers!

3. *Real objections*. Real objections are the actual concerns a buyer has about a potential purchase. They are often hidden behind smokescreens.

Consider the following story reported by a hiring manager:

We had finally found an excellent candidate for a technical manager's position. We made an offer, but he wanted time to think it over. A short while later we found out that he had been simultaneously talking with another employer nearer to his home. In the final analysis, he turned us down because of traffic congestion. We didn't offer enough of an advantage to overcome his objection to the daily traffic jam in our area.

In essence, this candidate was saying that he *wouldn't do* what it took to work for this employer, given that he had a choice. If this hiring manager had been able to bring the candidate's objections out from behind the smokescreen, some solution might have been worked out earlier.

Consider another case:

> Getting people to relocate to our area from some other areas is nearly impossible. People literally have to trade an estate for an apartment. We have to either pay them far more than we planned, or we have to be less choosy about their skills.

In other words, qualified candidates say that they *can't afford* to take these jobs. They consider the trade-offs too great. How can you handle real objections such as these? Here are some key points:

- Present your employment strengths and weaknesses only to *acceptable* applicants. You want to bring each acceptable candidate to the same point in the employment process. If your top candidate rejects your employment offer, you are positioned to proceed immediately to the next.

- When you review negatives and potential drawbacks with the candidate, ask for his or her reaction. This gives you the information you need to overcome objections.

- When discussing weaknesses and drawbacks, it is important not only to be truthful about them but also to describe what the company has done or will do in the future to improve things.

- Summarize the information you obtained during the earlier steps of the interview, in which you became convinced that the person is qualified.

    This is your opportunity to highlight the matches between the candidate's qualifications and your own requirements.

    For example, after describing a potential negative differentiator, you might point out something like: "Although some of our employees have found this troublesome, my interpretation of your experience and employment needs suggests that you are accustomed to this sort of work setting. When you told me about (something the candidate said that indicated self-sufficiency), I concluded that you would enjoy working here. How do you feel about that?"

If, on the other hand, you have reservations about your candidate's ability to cope with a highly self-sufficient environment, you might say: "I'm a little concerned about one of your earlier answers. I want to discuss it so we don't have any misunderstanding. When I asked you about your 'ideal work environment', you told me you work best when your manager gives you specific steps to follow. You described a printed 'troubleshooting guide' everybody kept at their work stations. Our managers always try to make their expectations and work goals clear, but they would be very unlikely to write down the specific steps involved."

And again, you would then follow up your observations with a series of questions, such as: "Do you think you would like to work in the kind of environment we have here? Have you worked under similar conditions somewhere else?"

- End the interview by describing the employment features that match the candidate's desired benefits. Select especially those areas where you can position yourself most strongly against your employment competition.

  Some employers might make a "trial" offer at the end of the interview, similar to the "trial close" that salespeople use to test a buyer's seriousness. For employment purposes, such an offer would necessarily be tentative, subject to verification of references and other information shared during the interview.

Remember that candidates have greater control over their decision-making if they have sufficient information. An exchange of information sets realistic expectations and forms the basis for an adult-to-adult relationship from the first day. It is yet another step on the road to successful competitive employment.

Notes

1. Society for Industrial and Organizational Psychology, *Principles for the Validation and Use of Personnel Selection Procedures*, 3rd ed., 1987. The SIOP administrative address changes every year. The current address is SIOP Administrative Offices, 617 East Golf Road, Suite 309, Arlington Heights IL 60005.
2. L. W. Seberhagen, "How Difficult Is It to Conduct a Validation Study?" in Society for Industrial and Organizational Psychology, *The Industrial-Organizational Psychologist* 28 (July 1990), pp. 41–46.
3. Ibid.
4. Questions are taken from the *Interviewer's Question Manual* (Norwalk, Conn.: Performance Programs, 1989).

7

Treat New Employees like New Customers

M any companies give special attention to first-time customers. This postsale support serves two purposes. It promotes a successful first-time experience, and it helps reduce buyer's remorse. This applies to the fifth step to competitive employment. If you would be retention-oriented, begin by treating new employees like new customers.

Buyer's remorse is a fact of human nature. After making a purchasing decision of almost any size, buyers wonder if it was the right decision. The bigger the buying decision, the more likely it is that they'll wonder. Buyer's remorse is an uncomfortable mental state, characterized by contradictory thoughts. Buyer's remorse is related to what psychologist Leon Festinger researched as "cognitive dissonance" in the 1950s. The existence of two opposing potential results ("this was a good purchase" or "this was a bad purchase") causes people discomfort. People work at reducing the discomfort, and they work to reduce it quickly.

They are likely to feel uncertain, and the larger the purchase, the more uncertain they probably feel. New customers naturally hope for a positive experience, but they are often afraid they'll get the opposite. They may be self-conscious, afraid of embarrassment as they try out their new purchase.

The moment someone's employment begins, the potential for buyer's remorse arises. New employees are a type of new customer. They are hoping for a positive experience too. Curiosity and energy are at peak levels. Competitive managers know that this is a key time to set the tone of the employment relationship.

The two most common new-employee activities are formal orientation and training. Orientation sets up expectations and avoids misunderstandings. Training strengthens the skills needed to achieve early productivity. Both of these are worthwhile goals, but competitive employers know they can serve another purpose as well.

Careful orientation is a continuation of the marketing process that began with recruiting. There is nothing more disconcerting to a new buyer than to feel "dropped" by the salesperson soon after the sale is complete. Likewise, there is nothing more disconcerting to a new staff member than to be given a few quick introductions and put right to work.

Think of your own concerns as a buyer immediately after making a major purchase. Depending, of course, on the particular product you have bought, some of your questions might include:

- How does it work?

- How fast can I get it to perform?

- What do I have to do to keep it from breaking or being damaged?

- How do I care for it appropriately?

- How can I keep from embarrassing myself the first time I use it?

- How can I keep from hurting myself or someone else the first time I use it?

These questions are usually short-lived. A few tries with the new purchase answer the questions. The new buyer's goal is to get past the initiation quickly—to get "into production."

At some companies, the first day on the job consists of filling out forms, taking a short tour, making a few introductions, and then "getting to work." This works against human nature and stokes the coals of buyer's remorse.

Of course, the manager who has just hired a new employee goes through the new-customer state of mind as well, including buyer's remorse. He or she asks many of the same questions: "Did I make the right decision?" "Will this person work out?" But the difference is that the manager has control of initiation.

In the next two sections, we consider the marketing roles of orientation and training.

Orientation for Competitive Employers

To acknowledge the new-customer needs of new employees, rethink the orientation process, as you rethought the interviewing process in the last chapter. You are once again both a customer and a supplier. You are a customer for the new person's services. You have a need for them to impress you. At the same time, they have a need to feel they made the right decision.

Think of orientation in two parts—one part serves the needs of the employer, the other part serves the needs of the new person. We refer to the first one as company-centered, and to the second one as employee-centered. Both are important, and they are summarized in table 7–1.

Table 7–1
Orientation Topics

Critical Company-Centered Topics

These topics are critical to immediate performance and should be covered at orientation.

- Necessities. These might include items of safety and confidentiality, and security and emergency procedures. In addition, they might include completing government and insurance forms, as required on the first day of employment.

Less Critical Company-Centered Topics

Theses topics are less important to immediate performance, and many companies prefer to cover them at later time.

- Organization charts, particularly if they refer to remote parts of the organization.
- The use of forms and the less essential procedural guidelines, as well as other noncritical administrative requirements.
- Detailed information about the more complicated, but less critical benefit programs for most employees, such as stock purchase plans.
- Career, education, and promotion opportunities, and how to get them.

Employee-Centered Topics

- The company's history, progress, goals. These topics can encourage the beginning of a "team" sense.
- Key employee administrative procedures, such as payday, how to enroll in the basic insurance programs, procedures for sick days, holiday and vacation

Table 7–1 (Continued)
Orientation Topics

policies, and the like. (Detailed information and descriptions of more complex programs are best discussed later.)

- Traditional orientation activities, such as the building tour, parking rules, cafeteria, introductions to co-workers, and so on.

- The unwritten rules. Allow the new employee to observe the company in action on such issues as dress, work hours, and other areas where unwritten rules are "in effect." Sometimes a panel of current employees can provide such information and answer questions most effectively.

- Manager expectations. Encourage a clear discussion of the manager's expectations of the new employees. At a minimum, you want to clarify your objectives, generally through discussion of a job description. The discussion should include any milestones that the employee need be aware of, such as three-month evaluations or competencies that must be mastered within a certain time frame.

- Provide copies of most recent employee newsletters, magazines, and the like.

- Distribute a written copy of the employee handbook for review and later discussion.

Company-Centered Orientation

There are usually two key items on the employer's agenda for a new employee. The first set is relatively simple, "housekeeping" type matters, usually addressing administrative, legal and security topics. Insurance forms, confidentiality agreements, defining important safety rules and the like are all important here. The second key item relates to the hiring manager's own "new customer" process. He or she wants to know they made the right decision.

Employee-Centered Orientation

New workers, on the other hand, have a different agenda. First, they want to make a good first impression by not making any embarrassing mistakes. Second, they want to feel they made the right decision in joining your company. Answering questions and concerns about these two issues should drive this portion of your orientation process.

How should you structure orientation? Many companies begin with what they want to cover first—the company-centered topics.

However, this works against a fundamental learning principle: People learn best when they think the information is important. Providing them with information before showing them why and how it is important is simply a waste of time.

Although you must cover safety requirements and other critical procedures immediately, other company-centered information is of far less interest at first.

The competitive employment approach to orientation, as in other areas, begins with understanding employee needs and the employee viewpoint. Therefore it is important to cover what new employees think is most important first. Furthermore, without any actual job experience or firsthand observation or participation in the work, many employees won't see the need for some of the policies or required procedures you describe.

Therefore it might be better to begin with your employee-centered topics first, followed later by essential company-centered topics, and possibly followed later still by less essential administrative topics. Aside from allowing new employees time to absorb and learn all they need to know, scheduling a series of shorter orientation sessions can help build camaraderie and a sense of team spirit in the group.

There is a second benefit to holding several short orientations instead of a single long one. Follow-up sessions can help you determine how well a new employee feels things are going. It allows plenty of time for the employee to decide how he or she feels, and yet you can still do something to rectify problems. A follow-up orientation session is your opportunity to clear up any miscommunications, as well as to discuss any misperceptions on the part of the employee.

The best orientation programs are standardized. Both large and small companies have something to gain in following a standard flow. Standardization assures that new employees are given equal information on items that concern everyone. In addition, standardization reduces the effort that the individual who provides the orientation must expend. This will help to ensure that the orientation is actually done and that it is done consistently.

Table 7–2 summarizes some of the most common mistakes employers make in orientations.

Table 7–2
Most Commonly Made Orientation Mistakes

Mistake 1. Give more orientation to some employees than to others.

Mistake 2. Have a nonstandardized orientation, defined by departments or managers.

Mistake 3. Skip orientation altogether.

Mistake 4. Focus only on what the company wants the employee to know and ignore what the employee wants to know.

Mistake 5. Assume that employees will be oriented by the manager.

Mistake 6. Orientation overkill—overloading the orientation with more information than a person can absorb at one time.

It is critically important that both employer and employee have clear expectations of each other. The responsibility for making this happen falls on the employer's shoulders more than the employee's. Unfortunately, the traditional view is that the employee must understand and accommodate the employer—but not the other way around. Therefore, most discussions between a manager and a new hire wrongly center on the manager's needs.

If the interview was conducted effectively, you already have information about the employee's "total employment" expectations. To help you understand the motivational profile of your new employee, you could examine your interview questions on employee motivations. There are some new tests and surveys emerging to help new manager/employee teams communicate with each other.[1]

If you would want your new hires to have a positive new-customer experience, orient them as you would new customers.

New-Employee Training Is Like New-Customer Training

Most major or complex purchases require customer training, or at least a good product manual. A new stove comes with an instruction manual. An automobile salesperson may take a customer for a test drive, no doubt showing off some of the new car's features. A computer salesperson may sign the customer up for an introductory session.

Trying Out the New Car

Starting a new job bears some interesting similarities to buying a new car, buying a new house, or making other major purchases. Curiosity and anticipation run high. There are lots of questions. You may be a little nervous.

All too often, though, employers ignore the fact that new staff members are going through a "new-purchase" phase. They can't wait for the new employee to get down to work. This is particularly true when positions have been open for a while and work has been piling up.

Employment Manager Jeannie D'Ambrosio saw that this problem was affecting secretaries in her company. D'Ambrosio recruits for CUC International in Stamford, Connecticut, where the market for good staff support personnel has been very tight for a number of years.

"Secretaries are hard to find, so the manager typically has a backlog of work on the first day," she says. "The manager says he or she can't wait for the new secretary to go through days of orientation. They're very anxious for the new person to get started."

In other words, the managers took the opportunity to "try out" the services of their new hires, but the new hires weren't afforded the same opportunity.

As a result, new secretaries experienced a level of frustration early on in their new positions. This contributed to turnover.

"We now have a 'buddy system' for secretaries where a new secretary is assigned to another experienced secretary for the first few days," says D'Ambrosio. "That way we can give the new person some time to get comfortable before they're exposed to all of the manager's priorities."

Do your new employees require training? The answer depends on many factors, such as the employees' level of preparation before coming to the job. There are two benefits to doing new-employee training. One is obvious, but the other may not be.

A trained person is likely to start to do a good job sooner. This benefits the company by raising productivity. It also avoids production, service, or customer contact mistakes.

The new employees derive a less obvious benefit. Anxious to please and hoping to avoid embarrassment, most people want to succeed quickly at a new job. When training helps them meet this goal, they are likely to have a positive new-customer experience.

Although nearly all new employees begin their work in a positive frame of mind, smart managers make sure that they sustain it. Training is one obvious way to ensure this result.

Training is most effectively provided before the person has to perform something. This may seem obvious, but it is often ignored. There is a fine line between offering training too early and waiting too long to offer it. Describing the intricate details of a manufacturing process to employees, for example, before they see the finished product or understand the overall operation might be a waste. On the other hand, don't wait so long to offer training that someone learns poor work approaches.

Many companies assess new employees' abilities for performing specific jobs before hiring them. If you have not, do so before turning the new employee onto the job. It's another way to assure that he or she will have a positive new-customer experience.

To summarize, the decision to offer new-employee training or orientation is much like the decision to ensure that customers appreciate their purchase. You want the customer to have a good experience with your product early in the postpurchase phase. As a by-product of this good experience, you hope to obtain repeat purchases, good references, and satisfied customers.

Consciously arranging for new employees to feel and be successful is another hallmark of the competitive employer. It sets up the right environment for ongoing employment relationships, which we'll explore in the next chapter.

Note

1. Paul Connolly, *Worker Motivation Profile* (Norwalk, Conn.: Performance Programs, 1990).

8

Be Retention-Oriented

Effective manufacturers and marketers keep their customers. Effective employers keep the right people. Marketers who are effective competitors know that unhappy customers are hard to recover. Competitive employers know that it takes an effort to turn around a disillusioned employee. Smart marketers know that the first-time sale is just an opener. They work to keep their customers, and they try to get them back if something goes wrong.

Retention is a process. It starts with recruiting and selecting the right people. It continues with effective management and leadership. It addresses specific instances when good people show signs of leaving. These points are key to the fifth step of competitive employment.

Retention is important in a tight labor and skills market. Keeping the right people helps reduce your exposure to the market.

It's key for you as an employer to hold down the problems that lead to turnover. Don't let negative situations force good employees to search for alternatives.

Some unwanted turnover is beyond your control. But many companies hurt themselves—and help their employment competitors—by chasing or driving employees away. They do it by committing many errors—but they do it most of all through projecting an attitude that employees are easily replaceable.

Managing for Retention

Before you can manage for retention, you need to understand people's main motivations for working. Seen through the "total employment concept" a few chapters ago, these motivations are

Table 8–1
Major Components of High Employee Motivation

Components Related to Work

Fair compensation and benefits
Job challenge
Job meaning
Opportunity for growth
Job security
Reasonable workload
Orientation to quality and success
Conducive physical environment

Components Related to People

Immediate manager's interpersonal skills
Immediate manager's functional skills
Senior management's communications
Organization's culture and climate
Opportunity for innovation
Co-worker cooperation
Employee involvement

like product attributes. An employer's ability to deliver motivating job attributes goes a long way toward retaining employees. While specific motivations differ from person to person, research shows that people's core needs are very consistent. The presence of these factors is positive, their absence negative. Table 8–1 shows key features that lead to high motivation.[1]

People evaluate these issues differently and often privately. The issues themselves may have different priorities at different times in a person's work life. The presence and positive quality of these attributes is a marketing issue for the employer. It's important, then, to look at the three most important ways to deliver them:

- Effective management and leadership
- Work structured to provide challenge, meaning, and opportunity for growth
- Fair total compensation

There are libraries full of books on each of these subjects. The bibliography refers to some of them. The rest of this chapter examines each of them briefly for their impact on the employment marketing process.

Effective Management and Leadership

Managers and executive leaders play critical *service* roles in organizations.

The most effective managers and executives, like good coaches, understand how to bring out employee performance by appealing to internal "hot buttons." If manager and executive services are inadequate, a work group is missing a critical service indeed. In a sense, management that fails to provide these services violates its part of the unwritten contract. Work group performance is often the first casualty.

Management Effectiveness. The job of a manager is to see that each task related to current operations is performed well, given the resources available. Good management is the result not of an attitude, a personality trait, or even a style. Instead, as many researchers have shown, good management is the result of doing the right things. The right behaviors for managers consist of a handful of key skills, as psychologist Clark Wilson and others have shown.[2] The most basic of these skills is the ability to communicate clear work goals and objectives to employees. After this ability, skills in the areas of planning, problem-solving, coaching, and feedback come into play. A third set of critical skills is maintaining sufficient positive drive and energy to make sure employees follow through. Finally, good management requires recognizing and rewarding good performance.

With great personal effort, you might be able to change your "management style." This presupposes that you want to do so and can identify precisely what a "change in style" means. You can much more easily change what you do in terms of your behavior than you can change your style. Changing your behavior doesn't require changing your style or personality at all. For this reason, most modern management training consists of a focus on the behavior of management rather than management style. Table 8–2

Table 8–2
Management Behaviors Related to Effective Organizations

The Management Environment

Orientation to the future
Sensitivity to the marketplace
Sensitivity to the organization
Standards of performance
Conflict management
Tension/Pressure
Respect for leadership
Trust in management

Employee Involvement and Commitment

Information Sharing/Feedback
Operational Support
Team Development
Managing Diversity
Reward Sharing
Opportunity for growth
Encouragement for quality
Loyalty
Commitment
Employee motivation

Note: Managers have profound influence on organization effectiveness. The above list, taken from the *Survey of Organization Values*, shows key areas of management performance. This list is designed to identify behaviors related to the Malcolm Baldrige quality program.[3]

lists categories of management behavior that contribute to effective organizations.

Leadership Effectiveness. A manager who supervises other managers has to be able not only to manage well but also to "lead a charge." Beyond a mere cheerleading role is the executive responsibility of identifying opportunities for change. Leadership skills are essential to bring about organizational change. For top executives and entrepreneurs, these skills are even more critical, for these people lead the charge.

As in management, behaviors related to effective leadership are key to improved effectiveness, not a laundry list of traits and characteristics that people in fact cannot easily change. This simple truth is probably even more obvious in the area of leadership than it is in the area of management.

When you think of an effective leader, who comes to your mind? American businesspeople often mention Lee Iacocca in this connection. In the field of politics, they mention Lincoln, Franklin Roosevelt, Kennedy, and Reagan. Those with military backgrounds mention George Patton, Genghis Khan, and even Adolf Hitler. In the area of social change, Martin Luther King, Jr., Gandhi, and others are frequently cited. Regardless of who you consider an effective leader, it is likely that in "leadership style," or personality, there is only one notable consistency among such people. They obtained "buy-in" from massive numbers of people and effected enormous changes (some for the better, some for the worse).

What all leaders have in common are some key skills and abilities. They all have an *idea* for change; *sensitivity* to how people will respond to the idea (and how to get people to respond favorably to it); and the *drive* and commitment to make sure the idea is successfully carried out. These three basics are what Clark Wilson, a longtime researcher in the area of leadership, has called the "vision, sensing and drive" of leadership.[4]

Certainly some personality characteristics can be assets or liabilities in management or in leadership. It is easier to lead if others see you as possessing a fair amount of charisma, for example. But leadership depends more on what the leader does than who the leader is. And this is very fortunate, since it means that leadership can be learned like any other set of skills.

Leadership and management are services to an organization. Performed well, they produce key ingredients in work team effectiveness. These ingredients are challenge, meaning, and perceived opportunity.

Challenge, Meaning and Opportunity for Growth

Presenting challenges is motivating for many people. It encourages them to develop new skills, and most people enjoy applying skills to accomplish something meaningful. Most people want to enjoy success in the face of meaningful challenge. Most people find that such challenge provides them with opportunity for growth—either through development of new skills or through promotions.

Providing employees with adequate job challenges is a key tool for keeping them engaged. One way to think about job challenge is to consider the gap between employees' current abilities and the demands of the tasks they are to accomplish. Too little challenge leads to boredom—and too much challenge leads to job stress.

Effective managers structure work so that an individual doesn't fall too far on either side of the stress-boredom continuum. At times, this means asking people to stretch, extending the gap between current abilities and job demands. In times of slower business growth or downsizing, the meaning of "stretch" might be less ambitious.

Some people are motivated by the idea that they can bridge large gaps between their current skills and the problems at hand. Many engineers are "problem-motivated" individuals, for example, thriving on the technical challenges of building new equipment or new systems. Employees who enjoy troubleshooting assignments are also likely to be problem-motivated.

On the other hand, some people are shy of work that forces them to stretch their current abilities. A classic example is people who like repetitive, predictable work. Their idea of a "positive" challenge is work in which problems to be solved are within their purview. Of course, even these people can perceive that their challenges are too little—which can have the same negative effect on their perceptions of their own work.

People are also motivated to do things that have meaning to them. If an employee sees no meaning in his or her work, an essential key to self-motivation is lost. The motivation to continue has to come from "outside"—and managers need provide its ingredients.

This is an inherently difficult task. It is far more positive to create situations in which people can be self-motivated. To do so, you need to know for each employee, "What is the meaning of *meaningful?*"

Meaningful work is work the employee sees as having a positive impact on something. This positive impact may be felt by customers, by other members of the work group, or by society as a whole.

In addition, many people find more meaning in work that exercises their skills. Such work provides them with a better chance at positive feedback. It offers an opportunity for growth through the further development of their skills.

Imagine a work team made up of people who feel challenged, who see their work as meaningful, and who see a future in furthering their skills. This group would be the most easily motivated and secure group that you could hope to have. Your job would be largely to define their work and stay out of the way.

Many employees regard opportunities for growth as synonymous with promotions and other career opportunities.

Those who manage in this area most effectively present employees with a realistic view of the work and of the likely opportunities for promotion, beginning with recruitment. Some employers conduct periodic employee surveys or other structured programs to determine how well the skills and aspirations of their employees match their own business needs and opportunities.

Three major techniques will help you enhance your staff's sense of challenge, meaning, and growth: job design, job enlargement, and job enrichment. They can be used separately or in conjunction with one another.

Job Design. One approach to providing "stretch" in an assignment is to examine its structure. The earliest such examinations were "time and motion" studies of the efficiencies of various worker movements. These studies were often intended and used to improve efficiency with machinery or equipment. The basic assumption was that efficient work environments and procedures could increase productivity.

The "time and motion" approach is not always desirable from a motivational point of view. It sometimes leads to oversimplified or overstructured work. While simplification may reduce errors that result from distractions, for example, it can unwittingly increase errors that result from boredom.

The "time and motion" approach is still in use today, but its most successful applications are usually those used in conjunction with job enlargement or job enrichment.

Job Enlargement. In this enhancement technique, new tasks or job demands are added to an already established job. This approach aims to make the job more complete. The person whose job has been enlarged may come to be involved more with an entire process than with a few of its tasks. As with job design, job enlargement can also result in unanticipated difficulties. As one secretary in a newly "flattened" organization told us, "adding a new boring task to the drudgery that is already there isn't my idea of a promotion."

Job Enrichment. Many human resources professionals today prefer this technique to the other two. Job enrichment gives individuals more control over the planning, execution, and structure of their jobs.

In practice, job enrichment provides more direct feedback and "customer" contacts, external as well as internal. The work itself then takes on more meaning for the employee because it is connected to someone who is a crucial, interested consumer of it.

The bibliography lists several references that contain more information on these broad suggestions. The works of Frederick Herzberg and J. Richard Hackman are especially useful in this regard.

Fair Compensation

Price is a key marketing issue. Competitive prices can attract new customers, just as inappropriate prices can drive away even the most loyal customers.

Pricing strategies can't solve all marketing problems; nor can compensation strategies solve all employee recruiting and retention problems. Less isn't always better in pricing, and more isn't always better in compensation. Without providing the right compensation, however, you'll be fueling dissatisfaction and it will be difficult for you to maintain your work force.

Compensation and Motivation. To understand the role of compensation in competitive employment, it's useful to examine the theories of psychologist Frederick Herzberg. Herzberg categorized

Guidelines for Challenging and Meaningful Work[5]

Motivation research provides guidelines on how to fulfill people's need for meaningful work, challenge, and opportunities for growth. In general, a motivating situation is set up by providing the following in your work environment:

1. Provide a clear description of what should be accomplished, and make sure the description is understood.
2. Provide "whole" work assignments whenever possible. These are assignments that begin with basic elements or ingredients and result in "completion" of a recognized product or service.
3. Remove artificial controls over employees, and increase their accountability for the quality and quantity of their work output.
4. Provide employees with the freedom to adapt or change the work procedures as much as possible.
5. Provide direct feedback on product and service outcome whenever possible—from a customer. The customer may be internal to the company or external. If direct feedback is not possible, provide feedback through an absolute minimum possible number of middlemen.
6. Encourage employees to assume new and more challenging assignments. Reward those who do.
7. Give work assignments that deepen and broaden functional or technical expertise.

the sources of motivation as "intrinsic" and "extrinsic." Pay is an extrinsic motivator. Challenge and meaning are intrinsic motivators.

Herzberg compared extrinsic motivators like pay to a battery, an outside source of energy. As long as the battery provides the "juice," the employee will be "not dissatisfied." When the battery runs down, extrinsic issues can be a great source of dissatisfaction. Therefore, management has to keep recharging the battery. Employees take pay raises and new benefits for granted after a short while.[6]

Herzberg suggests that managers use a motivational strategy that balances pay (and other extrinsic motivators) with intrinsic motivators.

- Make sure people are not discouraged or demotivated. Provide them with competitive salary, benefits, and working conditions.

- Provide opportunities for employees to be motivated or encouraged through an internal sense of accomplishment, personal growth, and responsibility.

Some customers, to be sure, won't buy your product at any price. And some employees won't be motivated at any wage. Competitive employers see compensation for what it is—one of many factors that can help create a successful working relationship.

Determining Fair Compensation. Job evaluation is one of the most accurate and most widely used methods of determining employees' total pay. It is similar to job analysis in that it looks at job specifications and requirements. The approach differs from job analysis, though, in what it measures.

Job analysis looks at the "will do," the "can do," and the "fit" requirements of a position. Job evaluation, by contrast, focuses on the degree of expertise, amount of problem-solving, and level of accountability in a position. In traditional job evaluation, the greater any of these major components, the higher the pay level. (Chapter 10 briefly discusses some new views on compensation.) A job holder with more specialized knowledge or expertise commands a higher wage. A job that requires more problem-solving requires someone who can troubleshoot and be flexible. Similarly, those employees with more accountability for results, as well as more managerial accountability, command a higher wage.

Pay is a moving target, so these efforts must be continuous. The bibliography suggests several works on this subject.

Turnover

Even if you've selected well and managed well, some good people will inevitably show signs of leaving.

Unwanted turnover has a sobering price tag. Michael Mercer, author of *Turning Your Human Resource Department into a Profit Center*, suggests using three categories of costs to estimate the financial damage that turnover does.[7]

- *Separation costs* include the cost of developing procedures, the cost of administrative overhead, and the cost of the time spent in termination procedures.

- *Replacement costs* include the costs of advertising and other direct costs of employment (such as the cost of recruiters and the cost of tests and professional evaluations), as well as the costs of professional and management time and the associated overhead spent on replacement.

- *Training costs* include the actual materials used in any employee training, as well as the salaries of the employee and the trainers during the training period.

Mercer estimated the turnover cost for a single computer operator in one company amounted to more than $20,000. Unlike Mercer, other researchers include associated items such as lost productivity as part of turnover costs. For them, the $20,000 loss becomes even greater.

Beyond its measurable toll, turnover also takes an indirect toll. It sends a negative message to current staffers. It scuttles your recruitment, employment, and training investments, possibly even before you have recovered their costs. It strains every system in the employment process—recruitment, selection, initiation, training, management, and leadership systems all have to work harder just to break even. It places extra burdens on existing staff members. Over the long term, unwanted turnover can help cause low morale even if low morale is not directly the result of unwanted turnover. "If everyone keeps leaving, this must be a bad place to work," employees who remain think.

If you think your company has a turnover problem, the four questions below provide the basis for constructing an effective retention strategy:

1. Do you really have a turnover problem?

2. Why have valuable employees have recently left your company?

3. Who's vulnerable now?

4. What positive action can be taken?

Do You Really Have a Problem?

Turnover varies by region, industry, job category, and profession. Thirty-three percent turnover may be standard for a particular position, while 5 percent may be normal for others. Still, reliable turnover norms are difficult to find. Furthermore, those that exist mask the real issues. Turnover is expensive, no matter what the averages. If you can beat the averages by keeping the right people, it's money in the bank for you.

The best turnover yardstick is one that measures whether you're losing people you'd like to keep. You can create your own measurement by looking at the characteristics of the people who have left your company, many of which are listed in table 8–3. If you answer yes to one or more of those questions, you may have a turnover problem.

Table 8–3
Determining Turnover Problems

Do the people who leave your company meet these descriptions?

1. They had access to sensitive or highly proprietary information (that is, they could be extremely valuable to your competition or who could even become your competition).	yes	no
2. They had specialized knowledge, skills, or abilities as a result of training your company provided.	yes	no
3. Their knowledge, skills, or abilities are in high demand.	yes	no
4. They had an especially rare combination of knowledge, skills, and abilities, a profile that is very difficult to recruit.	yes	no
5. They had a proven track record of accomplishment in your company. They were proven "doers" (and therefore had attractive "selling points" to offer other employers).	yes	no
6. They had a record of taking on new responsibilities and duties without being asked.	yes	no
7. They fit particularly well with other workers or with the demands of your business plan.	yes	no
8. For other reasons, they are very difficult to replace.	yes	no

Why Do Valuable Employees Leave?

If you are losing valuable employees, your next step is to ask them why. This question is often asked—but rarely fully answered—in exit interviews on the last day of employment. In these interviews, most employees don't see any benefit in bringing up conflicts or situations that soon will make no difference to them. Most people don't want to "burn their bridges" or risk losing a needed reference by making a full statement.

In some cases, resigning employees might not be immediately able to articulate the real sources of their decision. For these employees, clarity will come after they have had the benefit of some distance from the situation and can compare a subsequent employment situation with the one they left.

In fact, the most insightful conversations with former employees are held between one and eight months after they leave. (Before one month, many people are still confused by the emotions associated with leaving a company.)

Who's Vulnerable?

Once you have examined the reasons that you have already lost good employees, you are in a good position to spot those who are now vulnerable. Following these steps will help you spot them.

1. Identify which employees you are most interested in keeping. These may be so-called key employees—those with crucial skills or knowledge on whom your business literally depends. They may be employees whose specialized skills or knowledge makes them difficult to replace under present labor-market conditions. Or they may be employees who have a history of strong performance, who are easy to manage, or who fit your available budget. Whatever your criteria may be, the first step in turnover management is employment triage. You need to decide which employees are most important to you and focus your efforts on keeping them. Make a list of these employees.

2. From this list, decide which employees on it fit a profile similar to that of employees who have already left your company.

3. Examine the employment history from the perspective of these employees. What good—and bad—things have happened to them in the most recent past? How long ago did these employees receive a pay increase or a performance bonus? Has the company or manager recognized their accomplishments? Were there any surprises at performance-appraisal time? Has the level of job pressure increased, from these employees' point of view? Have these employees' jobs changed in any undesirable way? Have these employees experienced any personal conflicts with co-workers or with management?

Each of the incidents mentioned in step 3 is a potential source of positive or negative feelings about the job. If an employee's poor feelings are allowed to linger and fester, they can result in transferring his or her motivation to work into a motivation to find new work—elsewhere.

4. Alert your managers to the signs of impending turnover. Employees will provide plenty of clues about such a change, and

Table 8–4
The Telltale Signs of Turnover

- A change in any pattern of attendance, including:
  - A "morning" person showing up later
  - An "afternoon" person showing up later
  - Lengthier-than-usual lunch hours or coffee breaks
  - Periodic changes in lunch hours
  - A request to use all accumulated vacation time on short notice
  - Any other change in vacation plans

- A change in work habits, including:
  - Improved attention to appearance
  - Increased number of phone calls placed or received
  - A sudden improvement in performance without apparent cause, such as an employee suddenly on "best behavior."

- A change in "participation," such as:
  - Fewer suggestions to improve work
  - Fewer questions about work assignments
  - General "withdrawal" from day-to-day work issues
  - Reduced contact with other employees

managers can easily spot them once they know what to look for (see table 8–4). When two or three of these signals are present in an employee who is vulnerable, it is likely you are about to experience some unwanted turnover.

Positive Action

Sometimes, a "cure" that is provided late in the process of an employee's decision to leave can be worse than the disease. When a person already has alternative job offers, it is probably too late to do anything. Most managers are not willing to make a counteroffer in this situation for a variety of reasons.*

But you can take positive action before the turnover process gets to this point. Meet privately with the employee as soon as you suspect there may be a problem. Show appreciation for the person's accomplishments. Discuss the importance of his or her role in the company. State that you have just reviewed some of events, and mention your concern about the employee's reactions to them. Ask directly, "My real concern is, are you thinking about leaving us?"

If the employee says he or she does not intend to leave, then you can repeat your appreciation for their effort. You could also use this as a checkpoint to discuss plans and the employee's goals. Going back to the "total employment concept," you might use this opportunity to learn if the person's concept of their ideal employment situation has changed.

What if you suspect the employee isn't being truthful? At that point, there is really little else you can do.

But if the employee indicates, either directly or vaguely, he or she is in fact thinking about "my options," you have been given a rescue opportunity. Clarify the reasons. If the employee's point of view seems reasonable, decide whether you should make an effort to change the situation. If the employee's point of view is not reasonable, say why you think it is not. If possible, suggest a solution and ask if that solution would work. Encourage a new look at the decision to find another job.

---

*A recent study by Management Recruiters, Inc., asked this question: "Would you extend a counteroffer to an employee who has accepted an offer from another company ?" While 41 percent, a small majority, said "maybe," fully 36 percent said a flat "no." Only 17 percent said yes, while 6 percent didn't respond. "Experience has taught us that the practice of counteroffers is rarely satisfactory, either for management or for the employee," they say.[8]

Employment is a purchasing process, for both employer and employee. By hiring, initiating, and managing well, the competitive employer has an opportunity to allow high-quality employees to flourish. They realize the marketing impact of careful management throughout every phase of employment.

Notes

1. Paul Connolly, *Investigation of Components of Job Satisfaction* (Ph.D. diss., Fordham University, 1983. Available from University Microfilms, Ann Arbor, Michigan).
2. *Survey of Management Practices*, (Silver Spring, Md.: Clark Wilson Publishing, 1984).
3. *Survey of Organization Values*, (Silver Spring, Md.: Clark Wilson Publishing, 1990).
4. *Survey of Leadership Practices*, (Silver Spring, Md.: Clark Wilson Publishing, 1989).
5. Two resources for further information are: Frederick Herzberg, *Work and the Nature of Man*, (Cleveland, Oh.: World Press, 1966); J. R. Hackman and G. R. Oldham, *Work Redesign* (Reading, Mass.: Addison-Wesley, 1980).
6. Herzberg, *Work and the Nature of Man*.
7. M. Mercer, *Turning Your Human Resources Department into a Profit Center*, (New York: AMACOM, 1989).
8. CompuSearch/Management Recruiters, "Reaction to Counteroffers Uncertain," press release, Cleveland, Oh., September 1990.

9
Measure "Customer" Satisfaction

M arketers frequently survey their customers for their satisfaction. Managers and executives routinely evaluate their employees. Few, however, get formal feedback from their employees. If you accept the idea that employees are the customers of your management services, you ought to consider soliciting their evaluation. Gaining such feedback accomplishes two things. First, it affirms to employees the importance of their reactions. Second, it is a most effective means of encouraging management and executive development. Thus, it is a key portion of your competitive employment strategy.

Competitive employers pay close attention to employee morale and motivation for other reasons. As we discussed in chapter 2, however, good morale doesn't automatically lead to high motivation or to high productivity. Why, then, should competitive employers be concerned about it?

High morale results in low turnover. It also makes the work of management and leadership much easier. Employees who are satisfied are less likely to resist either management or executive initiatives. Poor management will certainly result in poor morale. Put another way, good morale is one result of good management.

Dr. Frank Shipper at Arizona State University demonstrates the relationship between good morale and strong management with a simple group exercise. First Shipper distributes a simple, five-question survey in which he asks participants to rate their personal level of morale in either a previous or current job. After he collects these answers, he has participants rate the effectiveness of the immediate manager they had in that job.

Those who report having had low morale also reveal that they had managers with gaps in key skill areas, such as setting clear goals and solving work problems. The respondents also report poor department results and low overall effectiveness. Those who report having had high morale profile their managers as effective and skilled in these very areas.[1]

Is poor management responsible for your company's feeling that it operates in a tight labor market? The use of employee surveys is one of the simplest and most direct way to find out.

Using Surveys Effectively

If you decide to find out where you stand through an employee survey, keep these key points in mind:

1. Ask enough of the right questions to understand the employees' concerns surrounding perceived challenge, perceived opportunity, and perceived fairness of compensation, and their views of operational effectiveness.

2. When in doubt, ask less-structured questions rather than more-structured questions. Less structure enables the key issues to bubble up to the surface. Always allow for written comments.

3. Asking the questions implies that you will listen to the answers and consider doing something about what you discover. If there are areas where, up front, you know you are not going to change, don't include questions about them in the survey. Asking for input is an implicit promise to listen and consider change.

4. Employee surveys are an excellent tool to generate participation and introduce positive change. But designing and administering the survey are just the first steps. The heart of the process requires the active participation of employees in reviewing and interpreting the results, then jointly developing recommended actions.

5. There must be a plan to follow up on recommended actions, and someone must be responsible for the plan. During the follow-up phases, do all that you can to push the respon-

sibility for making the changes as low in the organization as possible.

6. No manager should be punished for "bad" survey results—the first time they receive them. Save the sanctions for later, if the suggested and expected improvements aren't made.

In the most successful situations, surveys provide an opportunity to step back and examine the organization more objectively. Surveys can bring up issues which are otherwise difficult to bridge. The real benefit of employee surveys comes from the discussion that then follows. In the best situations, each department manager meets with his or her employees to discuss the survey results for the company, division, and/or their own department. The first step in such a meeting is to understand the results. The second step is to identify the possible ways to change things for the better.

Though many people would explain these four points in their own terms and would rank them in different orders of importance, they constitute universal themes throughout the literature on employee morale, motivation, and retention. Their fulfillment depends on many things, one of which is the quality of management and leadership.

Table 9–1 offers a simple employee survey that will help determine your "customer" satisfaction.

Table 9–1
Quickscan® Employee Survey:
Thirty Questions to Determine Where You Stand

To what extent do you agree or disagree with the following statements? Please use the scale below for your answers:

1: Totally disagree
2: Partially disagree
3: Undecided or neutral
4: Partially agree
5: Totally agree

1. The compensation we receive is competitive with that of other organizations.
2. Our benefits package is competitive with that of other organizations.
3. Our jobs are challenging and interesting.

Table 9–1 (Continued)
Quickscan® Employee Survey:
Thirty Questions to Determine Where You Stand

4. The work we do here is important.
5. The work I do allows me to build new skills.
6. There is great opportunity in this organization.
7. I am clear about what I need to do and how my job performance is evaluated.
8. People can be sure of their jobs here as long as they perform at or above the standards.
9. The amount of work required of us is about right.
10. The performance appraisal/evaluation system is fair.
11. Steps have been taken to make my workplace as safe as possible.
12. My work area is very comfortable.
13. Management allows people to solve work problems by themselves.
14. People in this organization trust one another.
15. People here are recognized for their contributions and accomplishments.
16. My manager is always helpful when someone approaches him or her with a work problem.
17. People are given the training they need to do their jobs.
18. People are given adequate feedback about their performance.
19. Senior management is genuinely concerned about the thoughts and opinions of all employees.
20. Management provides us with a clear perspective on the long-term goals and direction of our company.
21. This organization has an excellent reputation.
22. Management encourages different points of view.
23. Our current organizational structure allows us to be responsive to customers.
24. People here are given an opportunity to present and try new ideas.
25. People within our department cooperate well with one another.
26. There is a high degree of cooperation among people within our department.
27. There is a high degree of cooperation among people in different departments.
28. Employees are involved in setting their own objectives and goals.
29. People are involved in making the decisions that affect their work.
30. Overall, employees here consider this a very good place to work.

Source: Performance Programs, Norwalk, Conn., 1989.

Note

1. Dr. Frank Shipper, presentation, Clark Wilson Publishing Certification Workshop, Westport, Conn., January 19, 1990.

10
The Competitive Employer

C ompetitive employers are definite about the people they need in their organization. They are market-driven in their approach to recruiting. They are both selective and sales-oriented in their approach to hiring. They treat their new employees like new customers. They are retention-oriented once they have hired successfully.

These approaches may not be enough to deal with the myriad forces now impacting the employment scene, however. Figure 10–1, first presented in the introduction, summarizes some of the most potent external forces and your strongest internal responses. To reiterate, your strongest internal responses, besides competitive employment, are:

1. Compensation strategies
2. Training strategies
3. Alternative staffing strategies
4. Technological advances
5. Management of workforce diversity
6. Creative use of geography

The most competitive employers use these approaches in combination with those described in previous chapters whenever necessary. In this chapter, we'll look briefly at each of these other, often powerful approaches. The bibliography supplies a list of books on each.

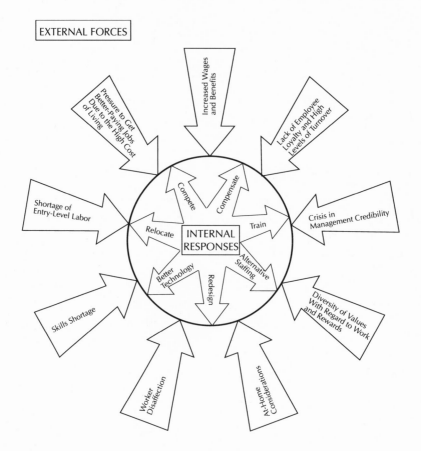

Figure 10–1. *External Forces—Internal Responses*

Compensation Strategies

Compensation can be a very effective employment differentiator. Some employers, however, act as if compensation were the *only* ingredient of competitive employment. "Skills are available if you pay the right price," they argue. These people argue that to draw top employees, you can basically take the traditional compensation scheme and raise the amount of money. Unfortunately, top wages don't necessarily draw top employees.

A simplistic, tactical use of pay may backfire on you. Among other things, it raises your costs of doing business without necessarily giving rise to a corresponding increase in revenue or productivity. If not handled correctly, it may also leave the wrong impression with some employees if it comes across as manipulative. Therefore, competitive employers have total compensation strategies. They avoid using compensation as a short-term tactic.

Traditional compensation schemes put managers and most professionals on salary, while other employees receive hourly wages. Pay levels are partially based on seniority and partially based on factors like span of control, level of technical or specialized knowledge, and seniority.

Tight employment conditions cause many companies to use alternative compensation strategies. Some recent examples of such strategies include:

1. Elimination of hourly pay schemes (putting everyone on salary).

2. Pay for performance.

3. Pay for knowledge.

4. ESOPs and other profit-sharing plans.

5. Bonuses, awards, and other recognition programs.

6. Flattened salary schemes, in which no manager makes more than a set percentage above his or her people.

If you choose any of these strategies, they need to be integrated with other management practices, such as goal setting, measurement, and feedback.

There are many arguments for and against using compensation as an answer to competitive labor markets. Many turnover studies show that pay is rarely the top reason that people leave an organization. If you pay fairly, compensation is usually a secondary issue in an employee's decision to leave. It becomes an issue only after some other event or situation causes an employee to start looking. Yet in some cases compensation is a key attractor, something drawing your employees away. Not surprisingly, compensation seems to be a more prominent feature in the "total employment concept" associated with lower-level jobs. In other words, the lower the job level, the more critical an item pay is.

A few years ago we conducted a turnover-control study for an area bank. At that time, several former bank tellers had recently left our client bank to work for the competition purely for a higher wage. In one case that higher wage was merely an incremental $0.10 per hour.

One of the tellers who left told us, "All of these banks are the same. Sometimes one pays more than another—that's all. Tell them I'll probably be back someday." There was no doubt about who was in control of the employment contract here. It was also clear that only one "difference" made a difference to this person—salary. She saw her bank employers as simple commodities.

Some salespeople, too, are highly money-motivated. And entrepreneurs sometimes cite their ability to earn money as a key reason for their starting their own businesses. Many companies have had great success with employee-ownership programs, allowing employees to participate in the overall profitability of the company. Many employees find their bonus potential a key reason for staying.

But the power of money, like the power of every other employment variable, depends on the individual. At one time or another, higher pay motivates almost everyone. If your recruitment-and-selection practices attract those whose primary focus is compensation, be prepared to manage your employees accordingly. The day a competitor outbids you may well be the day you lose that employee.

Training Strategies

Traditionally, most business training has been targeted to existing employees. Its purpose was to help them do better at their current job.

Training is now becoming something more—a key tactic for answering labor requirements. Training helps to "create" a pool of candidates. If you are unable to recruit and hire acceptable employees, perhaps you can recruit and hire employees who, with your training, will become able to do the job.

Employers have been using training as a part of their employment strategies in three ways:

- Developmental training for existing employees
- Pre-employment training, including various forms of co-op education
- Basic skills training, covering reading, writing and numerical skills.

Training is a benefit, since it fits with basic human desire for growth and future opportunity. In this sense, providing it fits with your orientation toward retention.

If you do provide some sort of training, what form should it take? Traditional training approaches that are long on explanation and short on practice might seem efficient, but they are generally ineffective. Some basic pointers on taking advantage of how people learn best are shown in table 10–1.

Generations ago, craftsmen learned their trade by serving an apprenticeship. A more senior craftsman would serve both as a model and as a coach. Learning would come when the apprentice, under guidance, would actually try to produce a piece of work. This very old training model took advantage of what has today been rediscovered, in an updated way. The key is that people learn by doing, not by thinking about doing.

Alternative Staffing Strategies

If you can't find or train the right people to fit your situation, another approach you can take is to change the situation. This approach has many uses in a tight labor and skills market. Some examples include:

Tiered Skills Arrangements

Sometimes jobs can be split so that less-scarce people can supplement or complement the more scarce (and often more expensive) workers.

Computer and software sales people who can handle the industry's complex high-end products, for instance, are scarce, and they are often highly paid. The industry now widely supplements its

Table 10–1
How People Learn:
Pointers for Effective Employee Training

1. Training must be meaningful to be effective. If the people you are training don't know why they're there—or if they don't see how the training is related to the work they do—you've got a problem.

2. People must be motivated for their training to be effective. Since motivation is an internal state, many believe that training should be offered only to those who want it.

3. Shorter periods of training practice spread over a longer period of time are better than longer periods of practice spread over a shorter period of time. Break your training up into short sessions.

4. If you are trying to train people to do something complex, break the skill into meaningful parts. Once the parts have been mastered, move into practice of the whole job.

5. Be sure to provide feedback. People must be aware of the outcomes of their efforts. We learn from both our successes and our mistakes—but only if we are given the chance to discover the reason for them.

6. Since people will always forget some of what they learned, allow them to practice well beyond the time they've apparently learned what they need to know.

7. The closer the training situation is to the actual work requirements, the more likely it is that your training will be effective.

8. Use positive models. A new employee often learns by watching a skilled employee do something correctly.

9. Encourage people to transfer what they have learned to actual situations. After perfecting skills in a protected or "classroom" setting, the new employee needs to apply them "for real." No matter how skilled the training, the actual demands are generally different and more complex than the practice situations.

sales forces with telemarketers. The telemarketers carry out the repetitive processes of cold calling and qualifying prospects. They provide field salespeople with this basic research, who then go on to fully develop the sales process.

The same strategy is also in evidence in other fields. The demand for paralegals, physicians' assistants, and lay ministers to supplement fully ordained clergy are all examples.

Nontraditional Populations

It's easy to see that many businesses are expanding their definitions of their target populations. Some recent examples include these population groups:

- Mentally and physically handicapped
- Homeless
- Retired
- People who require part-time work or flexible schedules, including homemakers and students
- Prisoners

Nontraditional Employment Contracts

Companies can respond to variable levels of staffing needs through the development of alternative scheduling and hiring arrangements. The most frequently mentioned include employee leasing, "permanent" temporaries, and use of staff "supplementals."

Technological Advances

Technological solutions to employment problems have long been controversial. Some people feel that technology eliminates jobs. The experience of the past thirty years suggests that, in fact, technological replacements for human labor create jobs for the providers of these products. The jobs they create, however, often require a higher skill level than the jobs they cut. Thus, in a way, they increase the skills shortage while reducing the shortage of semiskilled and unskilled labor.

This conundrum aside, technology can represent a viable supplement or complement to your work force. It is used in three ways:

- To delegate some jobs to machines.

- To remove boring, repetitive, or dangerous aspects of some work. These are often the most powerful applications in that they improve the quality of work life for staff members.
- To redefine entire processes and, in effect, redesign jobs.

Recent work-force uses of technology include automation of the following:

- Unattended computer center operations
- Fast-food self-service
- Automated telephone reception
- Supermarket self-checkout
- Automated coupon dispensing and redemption at supermarkets
- Videotape rentals from vending machines
- Self-administered credit-card payments for gasoline
- Automated telephone inquiry handling

Two factors should drive your decision to use these solutions: the financial payback, and the human element. The former is reasonably easy to calculate, while the second is less predictable.

Members of the computer industry have long known that new technologies often fail when users lack a sense of ownership of them. This is a valuable lesson for employers. In fact, some employees resist workplace technology precisely because the managers propose and impose it. Providing employees with a sense of ownership of the technology can make the difference.

Creative Use of Geography

Location is another way for addressing the employment issues at hand. The simple and traditional option here, of course, is to relocate the employee to where the company is located. While some continue to use this option, other views of location are taking hold. Three megatrends support these alternatives.

First, companies looking for people with crucial skills place more priority on those skills than on the employee's physical presence. Thus, employers are more willing to consider using people in other places.

Second, thinking has changed regarding the need to directly supervise people in the same place. As the master-slave and parent-child management models further erode, employers' willingness to work with independent employees will continue to evolve.

Third, computer and communications technology enables work that formerly had to occur at a single location to be dispersed geographically.

These trends have led to many creative uses of geography by employers.

Satellite Offices. One New York telemarketing firm has set up a telephone operation in a rural Iowa farm community. There, it largely employs members of farm families whose workloads are seasonal.

Telecommuting. This trend has taken hold in various forms. The most frequently cited kind of telecommuting is the combination of home-office work with regular but less-than-daily visits to the office. This option has been enabled by home computers, FAX machines, and modems. In its more extreme form, some people equip vans or trucks as moving offices, permitting them to work wherever they need to be at a given time.

Transportation and Housing. Various firms now provide long-distance bus transportation to bring inner-city workers to ex-urban locations. Some employers go so far as to provide weeknight housing for long-distance commuters. Hotel operators, in particular, provide living quarters for workers whose usual location is too far away for them to make a daily commute.

Location, like other strategies, is another piece in the labor-squeeze puzzle. While relocation is still a viable and frequently used option, technology and new approaches to management may be more practical.

Epilogue

The world of employment has become tougher, but employers are not without options. The most competitive employers will capture for themselves a major strategic resource: the right people to fulfill their business plans.

Of all the options and directions that are available, one is readily accessible: borrowing some lessons from marketing. This approach isn't always easy, because more than any other approach it relies on a set of attitudes that may be unfamiliar or uncomfortable in the employment sense. Moreover, this approach needs to be practiced at all levels, and it requires changes of managers and executives. Fortunately, the approach is relatively free of direct expense. Hopefully, we have shown that it can be effective in addressing each of the external and internal pressures of tight labor markets and finding employees for those tough-to-fill jobs.

Above all, remember this: When you've found a good customer, understand the differences that make a difference—and earn the right to keep the customer's business.

11
The Competitive Equation: A Self-Test

You've been reading about competitive employers in this book. If this discussion has made you wonder about your own company, this chapter will help you assess your company in competitive-employment terms. The following questionnaire will help you design your own competitive assessment. It draws on your knowledge of your company, your industry, and your region.

Internal forces that are at work in the employment scene are those that the individual employer generates. They include your recruiting efforts, selection and employment issues, compensation, management and leadership effectiveness, training, company climate, retention, and other variables over which you can exert direct control.

But employment competitiveness is more than the sum of an employer's internal efforts. It is also a measure of how effective those internal efforts are in countering the numerous external forces that impact every employer.

These external forces include the business environment itself, such as the general health of your industry, your market position, and other general factors. They also include regional and industry labor conditions, such as the availability of skilled people or people who are willing to work at a given wage. They include transportation and housing issues.

The Competitive Equation looks at both kinds of influences—the external, uncontrollable forces and internal, controllable efforts. If an employer's internal efforts are effective, they neutralize the impact of external forces on the company. Think of them as a ratio:

$$\frac{\text{Internal Efforts}}{\text{External Forces}}$$

The denominator is the sum of the external forces that are at work. The numerator is the sum of your internal efforts. As the forces in the outside environment add up, they can overwhelm the internal efforts you make. Put another way, as the employment environment gets tougher, you as an employer have to invest and improve upon your internal actions just to stand still.

How to Create a Competitive Equation

This questionnaire has two parts. Part 1 helps you identify the external forces and asks you to rate their impact on your firm. Part 2 identifies your internal, controllable responses. It asks you to rate their effectiveness. At the end of the questionnaire, you find your competitive ratio by dividing the external score into the internal score.

To get the most from the Competitive Equation, we suggest you take the following four steps as you fill out the questionnaire:

1. We offer a list of potential influences for each of eleven factors. Rate *each factor that applies to your situation* on a scale of 1 to 5. Not all factors will apply to your situation.

2. Add to our list other influences on your company. Rate these in the same way. You may use this as an opportunity to invite input from others in your firm.

3. For each major category of influences, make a concluding judgment about its overall impact on your company's effectiveness. To do this, average all the scores for that section. Note that part 1 and part 2 use different scales.

4. Transfer the ratings to the score sheet at the end of this chapter. The score sheet helps you apply weights to various categories if you wish.

Your final score sheet might look like this:

> Internal efforts score: 3
> External forces score: 5
> Ratio: .6

Scoring

The example above would mean that, based on your answers, your internal efforts are outpaced by the power of the external forces. A balanced score of 1 would mean that your internal efforts are well balanced with external forces. A score of more than 1 would portray an organization that is gaining forward progress against external forces steadily.

There are no right or wrong answers to these questions. It is merely an assessment.

Just as there is no one best sales, marketing, or financial strategy for all situations, there is no single best human resources strategy. But one thing is certain. All of your business plans must be linked to your competitive-employment strategy if you're serious about deriving the maximum benefit from your planning efforts.

How to Use the Questionnaire Results

Any self-assessment of this type is designed to help you get an objective picture of your strengths and weaknesses. Its value, therefore, is in doing the exercise, not simply in the final score. Just doing this assessment, you'll develop insights into why your company is feeling employment pressures—and then you can begin your discussions of what to do about it.

If you have the power and resources to change external conditions, it may very well be to your advantage to do so. Such action will benefit not only you but other employers in your area as well. Typically, though, no single firm can influence broad work-force conditions such as illiteracy, transportation conditions, and the like.

To take control of your internal efforts, we suggest you answer the following questions after you fill out the questionnaire:

1. Which external conditions are creating the most serious problems for the firm?

2. What options are available for reducing their impact?

3. If you took these actions, how would they change the Competitive Equation? (You can use the assessment on a "what if?" basis.)

4. What are the costs and benefits of taking these actions?

5. What is the opportunity cost of *not* taking these actions?

The Competitive Equation assessment questionnaire is designed to analyze a single business unit. For small-to-medium businesses, one attempt at filling out the questionnaire will probably reveal a great deal. For larger firms, you may want to try multiple passes at the subsidiary or division level.

The questionnaire can be applied to a single department or job as well. You can use it to help you strategize an approach to take for a particularly difficult-to-fill position.

The Competitive Equation is particularly interesting for diagnosing changes in the environment and their impact. We suggest that you use it on multiple occasions, particularly when formerly successful programs seem to lose their effectiveness. When that "ad that's worked for years" suddenly loses its zip, this could be an early symptom of a larger change in the environment, which requires a new response from you.

The authors are especially interested in hearing about your experience with the Competitive Equation for our own research purposes. Those who provide us with such information will receive periodic research reports regarding competitive employment strategies. A diskette version of the Competitive Equation is available. Send your experiences to Performance Programs, P.O. Box 105, Rowayton, Connecticut 06853.

The Competitive Equation Questionnaire

PART 1: EXTERNAL FORCES

This part evaluates the external forces at work on your company. These forces arise from competition, the government, the labor market, and the industry. A high score in part 1 indicates that your firm is under a high degree of external pressure.

1. The Business Environment

External Force 1A. The Market and Competition.

Market success and high levels of customer satisfaction both indicate a productive work force and have positive effects on morale. What are the positive and negative considerations related to your markets and customers?

1. Overall level of your customer satisfaction?

Very low	5	
Low	4	
Moderate	3	
High	2	
Very high	1	Score:_____

2. Market perception of your products and services:

Very poor	5	
Poor	4	
Average	3	
Good	2	
Very good	1	Score:_____

3. Overall market and industry growth:

Shrinking quickly	5
Shrinking slowly	4
Stable	3
Growing slowly	2
Growing quickly	1

    Score:_____

4. Your company's success relative to your competition:

Very low	5
Low	4
Moderate	3
High	2
Very High	1

    Score:_____

Other market-related factors that you feel should be added (write them in and score them using the scale below):

5. (write in)

Very low/very poor	5
Low/poor	4
Moderate/average	3
High/good	2
Very high/very good	1

    Score:_____

Add the scores for as many items as you have rated:

Total
Score:_____

Divide the total score by the number of
items you scored: _____

Average score for this factor: _____

Transfer this average score (which should be between 1 and 5) to the score sheet at the end of this questionnaire, for External Force 1A.

External Force 1B. Technology

What are the positive and negative considerations related to the firm's use of technology? Do most of your people see the use of new technology as a benefit or as a threat?

1. For your industry, the level of technological sophistication in your company is:

Very low	5
Low	4
Moderate	3
High	2
Very high	1

   Score:_____

2. For your industry, your people's comfort level with technology is:

Very low	5
Low	4
Moderate	3
High	2
Very high	1

   Score:_____

3. In your industry, technological change occurs:

Much too quickly	5
Very quickly	4
At an unpredictable but manageable pace	3
At a steady pace	2
At an easily manageable pace	1

   Score:_____

4. In your industry, there is a lot of untapped opportunity for productivity gain through technology and automation:

Strongly disagree	5	
Disagree	4	
Neutral	3	
Agree	2	
Strongly agree	1	Score:_____

5. What effect will new technology have on employee opportunities in your firm?

Very negative	5	
Somewhat negative	4	
Neutral	3	
Somewhat positive	2	
Very positive	1	Score:_____

6. What effect will new technology have on customers' demands
of your company?

Very negative	5	
Somewhat negative	4	
Neutral	3	
Somewhat positive	2	
Very positive	1	Score:_____

7. What effect will new technology have on the financial stability
of your company?

Very negative	5	
Somewhat negative	4	
Neutral	3	
Somewhat positive	2	
Very positive	1	Score:_____

Other technology issues (write in and rate using scale below):

8. (write in)

Very low/very poor	5	
Low/poor	4	
Moderate/average	3	
High/good	2	
Very high/very good	1	Score:_____

Add the scores for as many items as you have rated:

Total
Score:_____

Divide the total score by the number of
items you scored: _____

Average score for this factor: _____

Transfer this average score (which should be between 1 and 5) to the score sheet at the end of this questionnaire, for External Force 1B.

External Force 1C. Government

When a company's progress is partially or greatly controlled by the actions of an outside party such as state, local or federal government, employees can feel a lack of control. What are the positive and negative considerations related to government and legislative influences for your firm?

1. What amount of business depends on government spending that has recently been threatened?

Over 75 percent	5	
Over 50 percent	4	
30 to 50 percent	3	
10 to 30 percent	2	
Less than 10 percent	1	Score:_____

2. To what amount of regulation and regulatory review are your operations subjected?

Almost everything	5	
Quite a bit	4	
Some	3	
A little	2	
Very little	1	Score:_____

Other government considerations:

3. (write in)

Almost everything	5	
Quite a bit	4	
Some	3	
A little	2	
Very little	1	Score:_____

Add the scores for as many items as you have rated:

Total
Score:_____

Divide the total score by the number of
items you scored: _____

Average score for this factor: _____

Transfer this average score (which should be between 1 and 5) to the score sheet at the end of this questionnaire, for External Force 1C.

External Force 1D. Economy

What positive and negative considerations are related to the general and local economic conditions? How are employees and recruits going to be affected by economic changes?

1. Do economic cycles create uncertainty for your business?

A great deal	5
Quite a bit	4
Some	3
A little	2
Very little	1

   Score:_____

2. What is the current impact of economic trends on prospects of employment at your firm?

Very negative	5
Negative	4
Neutral	3
Positive	2
Very positive	1

   Score:_____

Other economic considerations (write in and rate using the scale below):

3. (write in)

Very negative	5
Negative	4
Neutral	3
Positive	2
Very positive	1

   Score:_____

Add the scores for as many items as you have rated:

Total
Score:_____

Divide the total score by the number of
items you scored: _____

Average score for this factor: _____

Transfer this average score (which should be between 1 and 5) to the score sheet at the end of this questionnaire, for External Force 1D.

External Force 1E. Media and Public Image

Positive (or at least neutral) media relations are a boost to recruiting and retention. What positive and negative considerations are related to media coverage of your region, industry, or company?

1. How is employment at your firm perceived by the public?

    Very negatively   5
    Negatively   4
    Neutral   3
    Positively   2
    Very positively   1   Score: _____

2. How is employment in your industry perceived by the public?

    Very negatively   5
    Negatively   4
    Neutral   3
    Positively   2
    Very positively   1   Score:_____

3. The public image of your hardest-to-fill position is:

    Very poor   5
    Poor   4
    Neutral   3
    Good   2
    Very good   1   Score:_____

4. Are past employees likely to spread negative messages about your company or jobs?

    Definitely   5
    Probably   4
    Neutral   3
    Probably not   2
    Definitely not   1   Score:_____

Other media and public image considerations (write them in and score them using the scale below):

5. (write in)

Very negative	5
Negative	4
Neutral	3
Positive	2
Very positive	1

Score:_____

Add the scores for as many items as you have rated:

Total
Score:_____

Divide the total score by the number of
items you scored: _____

Average score for this factor: _____

Transfer this average score (which should be between 1 and 5) to the score sheet at the end of this questionnaire, for External Force 1E.

External Force 1F. Raw Materials, Natural Resources,
and the Cost of Goods

Stability in this area, as others, has an impact on employment. What are the positive and negative considerations related to resources?

1. "The raw materials we need are assured."

Strongly disagree	5
Disagree	4
Neutral	3
Agree	2
Strongly agree	1

    Score:_____

2. "Our raw materials are very predictable and under control."

Strongly disagree	5
Disagree	4
Neutral	3
Agree	2
Strongly agree	1

    Score:_____

3. The cost of providing goods and services for your company is:

Growing quickly	5
Growing slowly	4
Stable	3
Shrinking slowly	2
Shrinking quickly	1

    Score:_____

Other raw materials, natural resource, or cost considerations (write them in and score them using the scale below):

4. (write in)

Very unfavorable	5	
Unfavorable	4	
Neutral	3	
Favorable	2	
Very favorable	1	Score:_____

Add the scores for as many items as you have rated:

Total
Score:_____

Divide the total score by the number of
items you scored: _____

Average score for this factor: _____

Transfer this average score (which should be between 1 and 5) to the score sheet at the end of this questionnaire, for External Force 1F.

2. Regional and Geographic Influences

Examine the regional influences on your firm's employment situation:

External Force 2A: Transportation and Physical Location.

What are the positive and negative considerations?

1. How attractive is your firm's location overall to your employees and recruits?

Very unattractive	5
Unattractive	4
Adequate	3
Attractive	2
Very attractive	1

    Score:_____

2. How attractive and comfortable is your current facility? (This may vary for office workers, factory workers and other groups at the same location. If so, you may rate each group's evaluation.)

Very unattractive	5
Unattractive	4
Adequate	3
Attractive	2
Very attractive	1

    Score:_____

3. How suitable is your location to your business purposes?

Very unsuitable	5
Unsuitable	4
Adequate	3
Suitable	2
Very suitable	1

    Score:_____

4. How much suitable public transportation is available to employees?

None	5	
A little	4	
Some	3	
Quite a bit	2	
A great deal	1	Score:_____

5. How adequate are area roads at handling peak-hour traffic?

Very poor	5	
Poor	4	
Adequate	3	
Very good	2	
Excellent	1	Score:_____

6. How adequate is parking (consider both availability and cost)?

Very poor	5	
Poor	4	
Adequate	3	
Very good	2	
Excellent	1	Score:_____

Other transportation considerations (write them in and score them using the scale below):

7. (write in)

Very poor	5	
Poor	4	
Adequate	3	
Very good	2	
Excellent	1	Score:_____

Add the scores for as many items as you have rated:

Total
Score:_____

Divide the total score by the number of
items you scored: _____

Average score for this factor: _____

Transfer this average score (which should be between 1 and 5) to
the score sheet at the end of this questionnaire, for External Force
2A.

External Force 2B. Lifestyle and Basic Living Needs

What are the positive and negative considerations related to local cost of living and other "quality of life" issues?

1. Considering your compensation levels, what is the availability of affordable housing within twenty miles of the workplace?

None	5	
A little	4	
Some	3	
Quite a bit	2	
A great deal	1	Score:_____

2. What is the availability of affordable housing within reasonable commuting distance?

None	5	
A little	4	
Some	3	
Quite a bit	2	
A great deal	1	Score:_____

3. What is the cost of living within your commuting area?

Very high	5	
High	4	
Moderate	3	
Low	2	
Very low	1	Score:_____

4. How consistent are employee interests and attitudes with those of the local community?

No consistency at all	5	
Not very consistent	4	
Somewhat consistent	3	
Quite consistent	2	
Very consistent	1	Score:_____

5. "People from other parts of the country consider this a desirable area to live."

Strongly disagree	5
Disagree	4
Neutral	3
Agree	2
Strongly agree	1

Score:_____

Other lifestyle and basic living considerations (write them in and score them using the scale below):

6. (write in)

Very unfavorable	5
Unfavorable	4
Neutral	3
Favorable	2
Very favorable	1

Score:_____

Add the scores for as many items as you have rated:

Total
Score:_____

Divide the total score by the number of
items you scored: _____

Average score for this factor: _____

Transfer this average score (which should be between 1 and 5) to the score sheet at the end of this questionnaire, for External Force 2B.

External Force 3. The Labor Supply

What are the positive and negative considerations related to your company's labor supply?

1. What is the regional availability of qualified professionals for key lines of business? How many are available in the region now and would not require relocation?

None	5	
A few	4	
Some	3	
Quite a few	2	
A great many	1	Score:_____

2. What is the national availability of qualified professionals for key lines of business? That is, how many are available nationwide and would require relocation to work for your firm?

None	5	
A few	4	
Some	3	
Quite a few	2	
A great many	1	Score:_____

3. What is the regional supply of semiprofessional, support, and other nonexempt employees available for your firm?

None	5	
A few	4	
Some	3	
Quite a few	2	
A great many	1	Score:_____

Other labor supply considerations (write them in and score them using the scale below):

4.   (write in)

Very unfavorable	5	
Unfavorable	4	
Neutral	3	
Favorable	2	
Very favorable	1	Score:_____

Add the scores for as many items as you have rated:

Total
Score:_____

Divide the total score by the number of
items you scored: _____

Average score for this factor: _____

Transfer this average score (which should be between 1 and 5) to the score sheet at the end of this questionnaire, for External Force 3.

External Force 4. Employment Competition

In previous lists, you examined factors relating to your company, region, location and industry. Now rate some of the same issues for your employment competitors.

External Force 4A. Direct Competition

Other organizations represent potential choices for your own labor pool, including those organizations' current employees. Identify three or four companies who you feel represent your employment competition:

1. How well are your competitors organized to attract candidates, compared with your firm?

Much better	5
Better	4
About the same	3
Poorer	2
Much poorer	1

   Score:_____

2. What is the general public image of your competitors, compared with that of your firm?

Much better than ours	5
Better	4
About the same	3
Poorer	2
Much poorer	1

   Score:_____

3. How good an image do your employment competitors project overall, compared with yours?

Much better than ours	5
Better	4
About the same	3
Poorer	2
Much poorer	1

   Score:_____

4. In general, how would you rate your competitors' pay levels, compared with your firm's?

Much better than ours	5	
Better	4	
About the same	3	
Poorer	2	
Much poorer	1	Score:_____

5. How would you rate competitors' benefits, compared with your firm's?

Much better than ours	5	
Better	4	
About the same	3	
Poorer	2	
Much poorer	1	Score:_____

6. How good an image do your competitors present in the area of career growth and advancement, compared with the image your firm projects?

Much better than ours	5	
Better	4	
About the same	3	
Poorer	2	
Much poorer	1	Score:_____

7. How good an image do your competitors present in the area of overall job challenge, compared with the image your firm projects?

Much better than ours	5	
Better	4	
About the same	3	
Poorer	2	
Much poorer	1	Score:_____

8. How good an image do your competitors present on job security, compared with the image your firm presents?

Much better than ours	5	
Better	4	
About the same	3	
Poorer	2	
Much poorer	1	Score:_____

9. Have you been the target of active raiding by your competitors?

Very frequently	5	
Frequently	4	
Occasionally	3	
Infrequently	2	
Very infrequently	1	Score:_____

Other competitive considerations (write them in and score them using the scale below):

10. (write in)

Very good	5	
Good	4	
About the same	3	
Poor	2	
Very poor	1	Score:_____

Add the scores for as many items as you have rated:

Total
Score:_____

Divide the total score by the number of
items you scored: _____

Average score for this factor: _____

Transfer this average score (which should be between 1 and 5) to the score sheet at the end of this questionnaire, for External Force 4A.

External Force 4B. Indirect Competition.

Indirect competitors are the many family, personal, and societal distractions that compete for your employees' time, energy, and commitment.

1. The level of substance abuse in your work force is:

Very high	5	
High	4	
Moderate	3	
Low	2	
Very low	1	Score:_____

2. Your employees request special arrangements or concessions to help them deal with their family responsibilities:

Very frequently	5	
Frequently	4	
Occasional	3	
Infrequently	2	
Rarely	1	Score:_____

3. The number of your employees who have basic skill problems (in reading, writing, arithmetic) is:

Very high	5	
High	4	
Moderate	3	
Low	2	
Very low	1	Score:_____

Other indirect competition issues (write them in and score them using the scale below):

4. (write in)

Very frequent	5
Frequent	4
Occasional	3
Infrequent	2
Rare	1

Score:_____

Add the scores for as many items as you have rated:

Total
Score:_____

Divide the total score by the number of
items you scored: _____

Average score for this factor: _____

Transfer this average score (which should be between 1 and 5) to the score sheet at the end of this questionnaire, for External Force 4B.

PART 2: INTERNAL EFFORTS

Part 2 evaluates the strength of your current position and strategy as an employer. Unlike part 1, a high score in part 2 is positive.

Internal Effort 1. Recruiting Efforts

What is your evaluation of your own firm's recruiting efforts?

1. How carefully targeted are your firm's recruiting efforts?

Very targeted	5
Somewhat	4
Generally	3
Not specific	2
As broad as possible	1

   Score:_____

2. How would you rate your firm's recruiting ads and other communications for their "candidate-centered" appeal?

Very candidate-centered	5
Somewhat candidate-centered	4
Neutral	3
Not very candidate-centered	2
Not at all candidate-centered	1

   Score:_____

Use the following scale for your answers to questions 3 through 7:

1:	Almost never
2:	Infrequently
3:	Sometimes
4:	Frequently
5:	Almost always

3. "We track and analyze recruiting responses."

   Score:_____

4. "We track and analyze the number of
   interviews required to make a hire."   Score:_____

5. "We track and analyze the number of
   job offers that must occur to achieve
   a hire."   Score:_____

6. "We know the sources of previous
   successful recruits."   Score:_____

Other recruiting considerations (write them in and score them
using the scale above):

7. (write in)   Score:_____

Add the scores for as many items as you have rated:

                                                  Total
                                                  Score:_____

Divide the total score by the number of
items you scored: _____

Average score for this factor: _____

Transfer this average score (which should be between 1 and 5) to
the score sheet at the end of this questionnaire, for Internal Effort 1.

Internal Effort 2. Selection and Employment Issues

Your selection practices have a lot to do with your overall employment effectiveness. Use the following scale for your answers to the questions in this section:

> 1: Almost never
>
> 2: Infrequently
>
> 3: Sometimes
>
> 4: Frequently
>
> 5: Almost always

1. Do your recruiters and interviewers critically examine and study job descriptions and make a thorough job analysis before recruitment?   Score:_____

2. Does your company use more than one selection method to evaluate candidates?   Score:_____

3. Are your company's interviewers trained?   Score:_____

4. Does your firm's selection process consider all three factors—skill, motivation, and fit?   Score:_____

5. Does your firm conduct careful and thorough reference and background checks?   Score:_____

6. Does your firm take the time to carefully screen everyone before hiring, even when there is pressure to hire quickly?   Score:_____

Other selection issues (write them in and score them using the scale above):

7. (write in)   Score:_____

Add the scores for as many items as you have rated:

                                                            Total
                                                            Score:_____

Divide the total score by the number of
items you scored: _____

Average score for this factor: _____

Transfer this average score (which should be between 1 and 5) to the score sheet at the end of this questionnaire, for Internal Effort 2.

Internal Effort 3. Managing New Employees

New employees are like new customers—they'll form impressions within the first half-day of work. Rate the effectiveness of your orientation process using the scale below:

1: Almost never
2: Infrequently
3: Sometimes
4: Frequently
5: Almost always

1. "A standardized orientation procedure
   is followed by our individual managers."   Score:_____

2. "Our new employee orientation materials
   are ready and are systematically dis-
   persed to our new employees."   Score:_____

3. "Experienced people who are doing
   the same or similar job as our new
   employee are made available for
   assistance and questions."   Score:_____

4. "We conduct a follow-up to orientation after our initial session and before
   six months have passed."   Score:_____

5. "Written job descriptions are given to
   all our new employees."   Score:_____

6. "Our new employees are provided with
   a formal performance review after
   their first sixty to ninety days."   Score:_____

Other considerations related to management of new employees (write them in and score them according to the scale above):

7. (write in)   Score:_____

Add the scores for as many items as you have rated:

Total
Score:_____

Divide the total score by the number of
items you scored: _____

Average score for this factor: _____

Transfer this average score (which should be between 1 and 5) to
the score sheet at the end of this questionnaire, for Internal Effort 3.

Internal Effort 4. Management & Leadership

Internal Effort 4A. Management Effectiveness

Rate managers as a group (or individually, if you are studying a particular job) on the following management issues. Use the following scale for your answers in this section:

1: Almost never

2: Infrequently

3: Sometimes

4: Frequently

5: Almost always

1. The managers establish clear work priorities.   Score:_____

2. The managers plan work and workload.   Score:_____

3. The managers solve work problems.   Score:_____

4. The managers provide adequate job resources.   Score:_____

5. The managers delegate to the right person.   Score:_____

6. The managers provide clear assignments.   Score:_____

7. The managers coach for performance improvement.   Score:_____

8. The managers make corrections effectively, when needed.   Score:_____

9. The managers encourage employee
   ideas.   Score:_____

10. The managers monitor work progress.   Score _____

11. The managers control work flow.   Score:_____

12. The managers recognize and reward
    good performance.   Score:_____

13. The managers control unwanted
    turnover.   Score:_____

Other considerations related to management (write them in and score them using the scale above):

14. (write in)   Score:_____

Add the scores for as many items as you have rated:

                                           Total
                                           Score:_____

Divide the total score by the number of
items you scored: _____

Average score for this factor: _____

Transfer this average score (which should be between 1 and 5) to the score sheet at the end of this questionnaire, for Internal Effort 4A.

Internal Effort 4B. Leadership Effectiveness

Rate the effectiveness of the leadership of your company—or if your are the leader, rate your own leadership effectiveness. Use the following scale for your answers in this section:

> 1: Almost never
> 2: Infrequently
> 3: Sometimes
> 4: Frequently
> 5: Almost always

1. The leadership recognizes valuable ideas.   Score:_____

2. The leadership is willing to take a chance on new ideas.   Score:_____

3. The leadership recognizes and responds effectively to internal company politics.   Score:_____

4. The leadership recognizes extent of its personal impact.   Score:_____

5. The leadership implements ideas with good timing.   Score:_____

6. The leadership implements ideas by working with the right people.   Score:_____

7. The leadership maintains high performance standards.   Score:_____

8. The leadership maintains a commitment to long-term goals.   Score:_____

9. The leadership maintains control over personal stress.   Score:_____

10. The leadership adjusts plans and
    ideas to fit changing circumstances.   Score:_____

11. The leadership persists despite
    obstacles.   Score:_____

12. The leadership recognizes the
    contributions of others.   Score:_____

13. The leadership develops the trust
    of the work group.   Score:_____

Other considerations related to leadership (write them in and score
them using the scale above):

14. (write in)   Score:_____

Add the scores for as many items as you have rated:

Total
Score:_____

Divide the total score by the number of
items you scored: _____

Average score for this factor: _____

Transfer this average score (which should be between 1 and 5) to
the score sheet at the end of this questionnaire, for Internal Effort
4B.

Internal Effort 5. Training and Development

Rate the company for its formal and informal training and development activities. Use the following scale for your answers in this section:

> 1:   None
> 2:   A little
> 3:   Some
> 4:   Quite a few
> 5:   A great many

1. Availability of formal employee-
   training opportunities.   Score:_____

2. Availability of opportunities for
   informal employee training.   Score:_____

3. Availability of developmental job
   opportunities.   Score:_____

Other training and development issues (write them in and score them using the scale above):

4. (write in)   Score:_____

Add the scores for as many items as you have rated:

                                              Total
                                              Score:_____

Divide the total score by the number of
items you scored: _____

Average score for this factor: _____

Transfer this average score (which should be between 1 and 5) to the score sheet at the end of this questionnaire, for Internal Effort 5.

Internal Effort 6. Company Culture and Climate

The underlying values of company management express themselves through what is commonly called the corporate culture or climate. Because the impact of such values is often more easily recognized when something is wrong than when something is right, the questions in 6A and 6B have been worded from a "negative" perspective. If you wish, you may reverse the wording of these questions to a positive perspective, as long as you also reverse the scores for the scale (for example, so that 1 means "Almost never").

Rate the direct and indirect effects of corporate values using the scale below:

1: Almost always

2: Frequently

3: Sometimes

4: Infrequently

5: Almost never

Internal Effort 6A. Work-Related Issues

1. Do the employees at your firm express the feeling that they're overworked?   Score:_____

2. Do the employees express disappointment at the amount of challenge in their jobs?   Score:_____

3. Do the employees express disappointment at the amount of attention paid to product or service quality?   Score:_____

4. Do the employees express disappointment at the skill level of their managers?   Score:_____

5. Do the employees express disappoint-
    ment at the lack of tools, equipment,
    or materials to do their work?   Score:_____

6. Do the employees express disappoint-
    ment at lack of support resources?   Score:_____

7. Do the employees express disappoint-
    ment at the amount of training they
    receive?   Score:_____

8. Do the employees express disappoint-
    ment at the amount of recognition
    they receive?   Score:_____

Other work-related culture and climate issues (write in and score using the scale above):

9. (write in)   Score:_____

Add the scores for as many items as you have rated:

                                                      Total
                                                      Score:_____

Divide the total score by the number of
items you scored: _____

Average score for this factor: _____

Transfer this average score (which should be between 1 and 5) to the score sheet at the end of this questionnaire, for Internal Effort 6A.

Internal Effort 6B. Issues Surrounding Work

What are the positive and negative considerations surrounding the jobs at your company? Use the following scale:

1: Almost always
2: Frequently
3: Sometimes
4: Infrequently
5: Almost never

1. Do the employees express disappointment at the support they receive from their immediate managers?   Score:_____

2. Do the employees express disappointment at the level or amount of information they receive from management?   Score:_____

3. Do the employees express disappointment at the amount of support they receive from upper management?   Score:_____

4. Do the employees express disappointment at the information they receive about how their work fits with the total work product?   Score:_____

5. Do the employees express disappointment at the level and amount of their job security?   Score:_____

6. Do the employees express disappointment at their physical work conditions?   Score:_____

7. Do the employees express disappointment at their compensation and benefits?   Score:_____

8. Do the employees express disappoint-
    ment at the level of cooperation they
    receive from their co-workers?   Score:_____

9. Do the employees express disappoint-
    ment at their future job opportunities?   Score:_____

Other indirect considerations in the culture and climate (write them in and score them according to the scale above):

10. (write in)   Score:_____

Add the scores for as many items as you have rated:

                                                  Total
                                                  Score:_____

Divide the total score by the number of
items you scored: _____

Average score for this factor: _____

Transfer this average score (which should be between 1 and 5) to the score sheet at the end of this questionnaire, for Internal Effort 6B.

Internal Effort 6C. Organization Overall

What are the positive and negative considerations in working for the company overall? Use the following scale (note change):

1: Almost never
2: Infrequently
3: Sometimes
4: Frequently
5: Almost always

1. Do the employees express pride or
    a sense of belonging with the company?   Score:_____

2. Do the employees feel they can
    express what they think without
    unfair consequences?   Score:_____

3. Do the employees feel they can trust
    company management?   Score:_____

4. Do the employees feel the firm is
    interested in innovation and new ideas?   Score:_____

5. Do the employees feel that manage-
    ment is interested in their concerns?   Score:_____

6. Do the employees feel that they have
    a relatively harmonious working
    relationship with their co-workers?   Score:_____

7. Do the employees feel they have a
    relatively harmonious working
    relationship with management?   Score:_____

8. Do the employees feel they have a
    relatively harmonious working
    relationship with vendors and
    suppliers?   Score:_____

9. Do the employees feel the company
   has a harmonious relationship with
   its customers?   Score:_____

10. Are the employees comfortable
    with the company's pace of growth?   Score:_____

11. Are the employees satisfied with
    the number and type of internal
    job opportunities?   Score:_____

12. Overall, how positive are the
    employees about the company's
    future as a business?   Score:_____

Other company culture and climate considerations related to the
organization overall (write them in and score them according to
the scale above):

13. (write in)   Score:_____

Add the scores for as many items as you have rated:

                                                       Total
                                                       Score:_____

Divide the total score by the number of
items you scored: _____

Average score for this factor: _____

Transfer this average score (which should be between 1 and 5) to
the score sheet at the end of this questionnaire, for Internal Effort
6C.

Internal Effort 7. Compensation

Evaluate the impact of your compensation systems by using the scale below for the questions in this section:

1: Almost never
2: Infrequently
3: Sometimes
4: Frequently
5: Almost always

1. Are pay levels within departments consistent?   Score:_____

2. Does your firm offer pay levels similar to those offered by other companies in your area?   Score:_____

3. Are your firm's pay levels similar to those offered by other companies in your industry?   Score:_____

4. Are the benefits similar to those offered by other local companies?   Score:_____

5. Are the benefits similar to those offered by other companies in your industry?   Score:_____

6. Can the employees earn bonus pay and other incentives for extra-ordinary efforts?   Score:_____

7. Do the employees understand how pay raises are determined?   Score:_____

8. Do the employees understand how bonuses and rewards are determined?   Score:_____

Other compensation issues (write them in and score them using the scale above):

9. (write in)   Score:_____

Add the scores for as many items as you have rated:

                                                Total
                                                Score:_____

Divide the total score by the number of
items you scored: _____

Average score for this factor: _____

Transfer this average score (which should be between 1 and 5) to the score sheet at the end of this questionnaire, for Internal Effort 7.

Internal Effort 8. Turnover Management

How well do you manage potential turnover? Use the scale below for your answers to questions 1–4 in this section:

> 1:   None
>
> 2:   A few
>
> 3:   Some
>
> 4:   Quite a few
>
> 5:   A great many

1. How many managers in your firm know the signs of potential unwanted turnover?   Score:_____

2. How many managers know when and how to handle employees whom they want to "save"?   Score:_____

3. How many employees would say that management makes a real effort to keep unwanted turnover to a minimun?   Score:_____

4. How much turnover does your company have in its hard-to-fill positions?   Score:_____

5. How much unwanted turnover does the company experience overall?

Almost none	5
A little	4
Some	3
Quite a bit	2
Far too much	1	Score:_____

Add the scores for as many items as you have rated:

Total
Score:_____

Divide the total score by the number of
items you scored: _____

Average score for this factor: _____

Transfer this average score (which should be between 1 and 5) to
the score sheet at the end of this questionnaire, for Internal Effort 8.

SCORE SHEET:
OVERALL EFFECT OF EXTERNAL FORCES (PART 1)

Transfer your scores for all the External Forces to the list below. Then, if you wish, rank them in order, so that those with the highest scores are first, and the lowest scores last. This will illustrate the forces that are creating the greatest external pressure.

1. The Business Environment

    A. The Market and Competition   _____   _____

    B. Technology   _____   _____

    C. Government   _____   _____

    D. Economy   _____   _____

    E. Media and Public Image   _____   _____

    F. Raw Materials, Natural Resources,
       and the Cost of Goods   _____   _____

2. Regional and Geographic Influences

    A. Transportation and Physical Location   _____   _____

    B. Lifestyle and Basic Living Needs   _____   _____

3. The Labor Supply   _____   _____

4. Employment Competition

    A. Direct Competition   _____   _____

    B. Indirect Competition   _____   _____

Add the scores for Part 1:   _____

Divide the part 1 total by 11 (or the number
of factors that you rated) to get the average
score. Your average score should be
between 1 and 5:   _____

Part 1 Average Score: _____

SCORE SHEET:
OVERALL EFFECT OF INTERNAL EFFORTS (PART 2)

Transfer your scores for all the Internal Efforts to the list below. As with part 1, you can rank the scores to get a picture of which efforts are strongest and which many need improvement.

1. Recruiting Efforts   _____   _____

2. Selection and Employment Issues   _____   _____

3. Managing New Employees   _____   _____

4. Management and Leadership
    Effectiveness

    A. Management Effectiveness   _____   _____

    B. Leadership Effectiveness   _____   _____

5. Training and Development   _____   _____

6. Company Culture and Climate

    A. Work-related Issues   _____   _____

    B. Issues Surrounding Work   _____   _____

    C. Organization Overall   _____   _____

7. Compensation   _____   _____

8. Turnover Management   _____   _____

Add the scores for Part 2:   _____

Divide the part 2 total by 11 (or the number
of factors that you rated) to get the average
score. Your score should be between
1 and 5:   _____

Part 2 Average Score: _____

SCORE SHEET:
YOUR COMPETITIVE EQUATION

1. Enter Part 2 Average Score
    (Internal Efforts) here: _____

2. Enter Part 1 Average Score
    (External Forces) here: _____

3. Divide line 1 by line 2 to get your
    Competitive Equation: _____

Your Competitive Equation can range from 0.2 to 5.0.

An Equation of 0.2 would indicate a maximum amount of external pressure with minimally effective internal responses. This is the "worst-case" ratio.

An Equation of 5.0 would indicate a minimal amount of external pressure with maximum internal effectiveness. This is the "best-case" ratio.

An Equation of 1.0 would indicate a balance, meaning that internal responses have kept pace with changing external pressures.

The key to improving or maintaining your competitive edge in employment is to watch for changes in the external environment. If these external pressures change or build, and internal efforts are not sufficient to meet them, your Competitive Equation can change very quickly.

Appendix
Overview of Major Federal Employment Laws and Regulations*

Although current application of federal, state and local fair employment statutes is subject to ongoing interpretation, industrial psychologists working in this area have come to determine the acceptability of specific job requirements after they meet a series of technical requirements.[1]

Determining Bona-Fide Occupational Requirements

The three informal "rules of thumb" presented in table A–1 may help you in your efforts to treat all applicants fairly. Their intent is to limit your screening efforts to most critical and legitimate pre-employment requirements.

Table A–1
Informal "Rules of Thumb" to Aid in the Determination of Employment Criteria for Job Knowledge and Skill

1. Will the person be required to know or to perform a skill in order to complete a job task immediately (the very first day) on the job? If "no," do not include this item.
2. Will the person always perform the task that requires the knowledge or skill under direct supervision? If "yes," do *not* include this item.
3. Will the typical new employee be able to develop the required knowledge or skill simply through doing the job in the first six months? If "yes," do *not* include this item.

---

*This material is informational only. It should not be construed as legal advice.

Table A–2

Knowledge and Skill Requirements for
Wonderful Widgets' Customer Service Representative

Basic Performance Requirement	1. First Day?	2. Under Supervision?	3. Six Months?	Pass Test?
1. Speak English in a manner understandable by both native and nonnative English speakers.	yes	no	no	yes
2. Write simple customer communications that confirm conversations or request additional information.	yes	no	no	yes
3. Be able to use a keyboard to input data to a customer support system.	yes	no	yes	no
4. Have basic familiarity with industry products, term-inology, and customer uses of specific products.	yes	no	?	no

Let's take a look at what Wonderful Widgets thinks are the most important performance factors for its customer service representatives. Widgets' review of the knowledge and skill requirements using these three rules of thumb yields the results shown in table A–2.

In table A–2 you can see that of the four basic performance requirements that were identified through the job analysis, only requirements 1 and 2 are true performance requirements. For Wonderful Widgets to hire someone with these two requirements, it will need to attract and select people who already have these abilities. In other words, these appear to be legitimate "bona-fide occupational requirements," or BFOQs.

If Wonderful Widgets were unable to attract such people, it could choose to establish an aggressive skills-training program to encourage development of these skills in applicants before hiring new employees to actually perform the work. Employment could then be contingent on satisfactory achievement of the necessary skills after completing the training.

In practice, many companies pursue both screening and training approaches as part of their efforts to meet their fair-employment objectives. Consolidated Edison, Aetna, and other leading companies have long had training and development programs to help the disadvantaged develop required job skills. In some cases, companies offer programs extending over as much as two or three *years* before releasing new employees to specific jobs.

Continuing with table A–2, you can see that requirement 3, a typing requirement, is likely not a true performance requirement. It appears that it can be learned simply by doing the job for six months. The typing requirement in this job is minimal, and speed is apparently not a major concern. Once again, though, Wonderful Widgets may want to prepare a new training program for employees, encouraging early acquisition of the typing skill desired.

Requirement 4 in table A–2 is trickier. Wonderful Widgets knows from experience that true industry "beginners" can take as long as eighteen months to learn what they need to know about their industry products, terminology, and customer uses to be effective in their work. It is probably safer not to consider this an entry requirement, although Widgets could probably "make a case" that such specialized knowledge is a legitimate pre-employment requirement. But Wonderful Widgets, like most employers, prefers not to have to "make a case" unless it is absolutely necessary. So it has decided that this particular requirement is something it can afford to live without.

By examining the knowledge and skills required to perform the customer service representative job, Wonderful Widgets will ultimately be able to answer this question for each applicant: "*Can* the person do this job?"

Equal Employment Opportunity Laws

Whenever a company addresses the topic of employment, of course, it needs to consider the role of Equal Employment Opportunity laws and regulations. How does a competitive employment approach relate to such considerations?

Selection and management of employees based on sex, race, religion, age, and other "group" identifications are explicitly illegal in the United States. Perhaps more relevant to our discussion, these criteria are *not* reliable predictors of actual job performance, anyway. Such factors are not directly related to skill, motivation, or fit. In short, using such demographic screening is the *antithesis* of competitive employment.

If you follow the principles outlined in this book, especially those in the following outline, you will be able to conduct a defensible, reliable, and effective employment interview that really will help you predict job performance. You will be able to make sound business decisions and find the best person to hire.

There are some common pitfalls, however, and we think it appropriate here to alert you to a few of them. Employment practices in the United States are subject to regulation by a variety of federal, state, and local government agencies. These agencies generally are charged with enforcing laws, executive orders, and judicial decisions aimed at ensuring equal employment opportunities to all members of the work force. These regulations, for which the various government agencies have enforcement responsibility, are commonly referred to as fair employment practice guidelines. It is important that you understand your company's policies and practices, as well as key requirements of federal, state, and local legislation that affect employment practices at your work location.

Interpretation of Equal Employment Opportunity (EEO) laws is an ongoing activity. Not only are new laws being written, but judges, through case decisions, interpret laws in differing ways. What was "assumed" to be legally correct prior to a court challenge may be changed as a result of a court decision.

The following two sections provide some information on hiring and the law. This is informational only and should not be construed as legal advice. The first section covers major employment regulations. The second section covers common questions and answers about Equal Employment Opportunity (EEO).

It would be impossible within the scope of this book to provide even a summary listing of the various federal and state regulations to which you, as an employer, might be subject. Not even entire books on this topic alone can accomplish that task fully. This is partly because of the number of such rules and regulations, and partly because individual rulings can drastically affect what was once an "accepted" interpretation of a law.

However, brief descriptions of some of the major government regulations should prove helpful, if only to reaffirm an employer's need for a legal adviser in many employment matters.

Employment Regulations

Title VII of the Civil Rights Act of 1964

The act prohibiting discrimination on the basis of race, color, religion, sex, or national origin is called Title VII of the Civil Rights Act of 1964 (amended in 1972). The regulations stated in this act are commonly called, with the additions mentioned below, Equal Employment Opportunity or EEO laws.

More recent interpretations also prohibit discrimination on the basis of marital status. The act covers not only the hiring actions of employers, but also the terms, conditions, and privileges of employment—in other words, almost any personnel action the employer might take. Recruitment, selection, job placement, training, promotions, pay, disciplinary action, discharge, layoff, and other conditions of employment are all covered by the provisions of this act. Private employers with fifteen or more employees, as well as all governments, unions, and employment agencies are subject to the provisions of this act. The act established the Equal Employment Opportunity Commission (EEOC) as the enforcement agency for these regulations.

Executive Order Number 11246

This order, issued in 1965, applies to federal contractors and subcontractors conducting work amounting to $10,000 or more. Essentially, it reiterates the Title VII restrictions, but it adds the requirement that these employers take "affirmative action" (that is, active, positive steps) to redress past discriminatory practices among the protected classes (by race, color, religion, sex, or national origin).

Vocational Rehabilitation Act of 1973, and Executive Order Number 19914

These two regulations extend the protection afforded the protected groups mentioned in Title VII and Executive Order 11246 to those with a physical or mental handicap. Discrimination on the basis of such handicaps is not allowed, and affirmative action must be taken to identify opportunities for those with such handicaps. The regulations apply to federal contractors and subcontractors, as well as to the federal government itself.

Vietnam Era Veterans' Readjustment Act of 1974, and Executive Order Number 11701

These regulations extend the protection of Title VII and Executive Order 11246 to disabled veterans and Vietnam era veterans. The regulations both prohibit discrimination and require affirmative action. The regulations cover federal contractors and subcontractors, as well as the federal government itself.

Privacy Act of 1974

This act gives employees the right to inspect, review, and change their employee records in order to prevent them from being misused. The act applies to all federal agencies.

Pregnancy Discrimination Act of 1978

This act prohibits discrimination on the basis of pregnancy, childbirth, and "related conditions." Most employers now treat pregnancy as they would any other medical "disability" as a result of this law. The provisions of this act apply to the same types of employers as indicated above for Title VII.

Age Discrimination Act of 1978

This act prohibits discrimination on the basis of age, specifically for persons between the ages of forth and seventy. The act covers the hiring process as well as pay, job placement, discharge, and other personnel actions. Private employers with twenty or more employees, unions with twenty-five or more members, and employment agencies are all subject to the provisions of this act.

Immigration Reform and Control Act of 1986

This act established a series of employer obligations to verify the employment eligibility of all current and any new employees. The act essentially forbids the hiring of illegal immigrants. Employers are now required to file a form (the Employment Eligibility Verification Form) to verify employment eligibility. All employers are covered by the provisions of this act.

Employee Safety and Health Regulations

Occupation Safety and Health Act of 1970

This act established safety standards for the workplace, and established the Occupational Safety and Health Administration (OSHA) as the enforcement agency. The law covers an immense array of workplaces and topics, and OSHA is continually issuing updated requirements. OSHA will conduct periodic inspections, allow certain variances from standards, and issue violations for anything beyond those standards. All private and public employers are covered by the current rules and regulations established by OSHA. The basic intent of OSHA is to *prevent* accidents and injuries from occurring. OSHA will provide employers with a wide variety of information and assistance to achieve this goal.

State Workers' Compensation Laws

All private employers in most states, as well as public employees in many states, are covered by state workers' compensation laws. The laws cover work-related disabilities. They can replace lost income, reimburse medical expenses, provide some level of rehabilitation support, and can provide lump-sum payments for disabilities and sometimes death benefits to survivors. Employees who suffer a work-related injury, illness, or death may be eligible for such compensation, but eligibility must be determined on a case-by-case basis according to procedures established by each state.

Pay and Benefits Regulations

Fair Labor Standards Act of 1938, as amended

This broad act established the minimum hourly wage and required overtime pay at a rate of one and one-half times the usual (base) rate for work over forty hours in any one week. Employers who engage in interstate commerce and many government employees are covered by this law. In most cases where this law does *not* apply, a comparable *state* level law takes its place.

The law defines certain jobs as "exempt," and others as "nonexempt." Generally, hourly employees are considered "nonexempt", and they are referred to as "nonexempt" employees in many companies. However, the classification of exempt or nonexempt is not always clear. Most salespeople are considered "exempt," as are some employees with significant management duties. Employers are well advised to seek legal advice in cases where the determination of status is not clear.

Equal Pay Act of 1963

This act prohibits pay discrimination on the basis of sex for substantially equal work. All employers and labor organizations are covered by this act. The clause "substantially equal work" is the subject of widespread litigation, and new interpretations are developed on an ongoing basis. A more broadly and liberally worded law covering the similar circumstances appears below, as a part of the Title VII regulations.

Title VII of the Civil Rights Act of 1964

This act prohibits discrimination in pay for jobs of "comparable worth" on the basis of sex, and it covers private employers with fifteen or more employees, unions, governments, and employment agencies. This is also a hotly contested legal concept, and the subject of new interpretations on a regular basis.

Employment Retirement Income Security Act of 1974 (ERISA)

This act established standards for employee participation in private retirement or pension plans. It applies to any employer with a private pension program. The act established standards of employee participation, vesting, and funding of the pension plan, and it is designed to make sure that employees receive the benefits due.

Consolidated Omnibus Budget Reconciliation Act (COBRA)

This act mandates that companies provide certain health benefits, including employees who have retired or been discharged, their spouses, and their children. The regulations also influence who is eligible for re-establishment of certain benefits upon rehiring. The regulations here are exceptionally complex, and it is another area where controversial and contested sets of regulations are evolving with new legal interpretations.

Labor Union Regulations

National Labor Relations Act of 1935 (also called the Wagner Act

This act established the National Labor Relations Board (NLRB) to assist employees in choosing a labor union. The act prohibits management from interfering with employee choices for representation by a union. The act covers all private employers and unions.

Taft-Hartley Act of 1947 (also called the Labor-Management Relations Act)

This act amended the Wagner Act and applies to all private employers and unions. Essentially it eliminated the strong "prolabor" bias of the Wagner Act, putting government in the position of neither discouraging or encouraging unionization.

Common Questions and Answers about EEO

Question: Is there a general list of questions that I shouldn't ask on an application form or in an interview?

Answer: Actually, there are very few questions that are expressly prohibited. Past experience suggests that questions or inquiries based on or regarding sex, race, color, religion, national origin, marital status, or physical and mental handicaps are the most difficult to defend.

An exception to this general principle is in cases where the employer can demonstrate a bona-fide occupational qualification (BFOQ). A BFOQ is any qualification or requirement that is in fact a necessary requirement for acceptable job performance. It is *very rare* that any of the categorizations above could be considered a BFOQ. One example of where sex might be a BFOQ is the job of restroom attendant. You will probably be hard pressed to think of many others.

Question: Aren't there some specific questions, though, that I shouldn't ask?

Answer: Some of the other areas and questions you probably should stay from would be:

"Have you ever been arrested?" What you probably want to ask, assuming your job requirements back you up, is whether the person has ever been convicted, not arrested. And even then you are safest to ask about only certain types of crimes that are actually related to the job. For example, for some schoolteacher positions, asking a question about previous conviction on child molestation charges is not only legal but *required* by some municipalities. The same question would perhaps be viewed as illegal if asked of a person applying to be a grocery clerk. Another question seen on many application forms is, "Have you been convicted of a felony within the past five years? If so, please explain."

"Are you married or single?" Asking this question would be hard to justify. What many employers really want to know is whether or not the job applicant will be able to travel, work unscheduled overtime, work different shifts, and the like. If those are legitimate job requirements, ask those questions directly.

"Who will take care of your children?" This question also may reflect a legitimate employer concern related to absenteeism or lateness. If you have determined that this is a legitimate job requirement for your open position, a safer approach would be to state your policy on absenteeism and lateness. Following your statement, you can ask, "Do you anticipate having any problems in being able to get to work on time every day?" or, "Have you had any difficulty getting to work on time in your other jobs? If so, why?" After all, not everyone with children will be late for work, and not everyone who is late for work is late because of children.

"Are you available to work on Sundays?" Again, the acceptability of this question depends on your particular job requirements. But stating simply that "Saturday work is required" is inadequate. Title VII demands that employers "accommodate" employees' religious observances or practices that place no real, undue hardship on the conduct of the employer's business.

"Do you have a high school diploma?" It's not a good idea to ask this unless you can demonstrate that this educational level is required for the job. You are probably less interested in the diploma than in whether, for example, the person can read. Not all high school graduates can read, and many people who are not high school graduates can read. Why don't you simply ask the question (or provide a performance test)?

"How old are you?" This question should probably be rephrased. Employers need to make sure that applicants are of legal working age as specified by your state. "If you are under the age of eighteen, can you obtain proof of your eligibility for employment?" might be a question more directly suited to your requirement.

"We'd like you take this polygraph exam." It is not a good idea to ask this. Pre-employment polygraph exams are currently against federal law.

Question: What do I do if information that I can't ask about is volunteered?
Answer: This is actually a very difficult situation for you as an employer. The burden of proof might fall on you later if an applicant charges

that information he or she revealed to you caused him or her not to be offered the job. The easiest way to stop someone from providing such information when you really don't want it is to respond, "I'm sorry, but is that something you see as related to your working for us?" If the applicant says "Yes," then let them explain. If they say "No," then change the topic. While it is difficult to ignore such information when it is offered, hearing it places an extra burden on you. Make doubly sure that you have job-related information to support your final decision on this applicant.

Question: Can I test for substance abuse?
Answer: This is another controversial area. As with all testing and pre-employment requirements, the employer must be able to demonstrate why such a test must be given. Legal judgements and opinions vary widely, even when an employer can make a statement about a BFOQ.

Other EEO Do's and Don'ts

- Your interview questions must be directed at gaining only demonstrably job-related information, and should be asked in such a way that is obvious to the applicant that the question is job related. Further, you must be consistent in your questioning of applicants. If you ask one applicant about a specific job requirement, you should ask all applicants for that job about the same requirement. For example, if the job requires overtime, you should not ask only women whom you suspect of having children whether they are available for overtime.

- Testing is subject to extra legal scrutiny. While the strictest rules apply to written tests, the regulations actually apply to all criteria, written and verbal, that are used to screen applicants. You should not design a verbal or written test on your own unless you know how to validate it. Validation involves showing the degree of the relationship between your performance measure and actual demonstrated job ability. For example, it wouldn't be a good idea to ask applicants to spell a word or read a paragraph as a way to assess their grammar skills.

- It is both the law and good business practice to make all reasonable accommodations in order to make employment accessible to handicapped people. Questioning applicants about their medical condition is usually handled through the personnel or medical department. After discussing the requirements of the job, you may discuss possible accommodations that could help the person perform the job. Such accommodations might include moving furniture, lowering a desk, installing a telephone amplifier, or adjusting the work schedule.

- You may not question applicants about their family responsibilities, plans, or marital status. Ask the job-related questions instead. For example, if the job requires working on the third shift, ask about the applicant's ability to work that shift—not whether they have family responsibilities that might interfere.

- Employers are required to make every reasonable effort to accommodate work schedules to the religious needs of employees, unless doing so would cause undue hardship to the conduct of the business. Be sensitive to situations where an applicant's religious needs might be a consideration. You should not, however, question applicants about their religious beliefs.

- You shouldn't question applicants about arrests without convictions, about arrests for which they have pleaded not guilty, or about arrests that did not result in criminal prosecution, including those related to military service. Applicants with criminal records should be considered for employment only after their criminal history has been evaluated.

- You may question an applicant with military service about military work or experience or training if it is job related. You may not make inquiries about the applicant's type of discharge.

- You cannot discriminate on the basis of sexual orientation in either employment or advancement considerations.

Note

1. *Principles for the Validation and Use of Personnel Selection Procedures*, 3d. ed. (Arlington Heights, Ill.: Society for Industrial and Organizational Psychology, 1987).

Bibliography

Employee Selection and Testing

Anastasi, A. *Psychological Testing*, 5th. ed. New York: Macmillan, 1982.

Arvey, R. D. *Fairness in Selecting Employees*. Reading, Mass.: Addison-Wesley, 1979.

Cronbach, L. J. *Essentials of Psychological Testing*. New York: Harper and Row, 1970.

Equal Employment Opportunity Commission. *Adoption by Four Agencies of Uniform Guidelines on Employee Selection Procedures*. Washington, D.C.: Federal Register, 43, 38290-38309.

Guion, R. M. *Personnel Testing*. New York: McGraw-Hill, 1966.

McCormick, E. J. *Job Analysis: Methods and Applications*. New York: AMACOM, 1979.

McCormick, E. J. "Job and Task Analysis." In M. D. Dunnette, ed., *Handbook of Industrial and Organizational Psychology*. Skokie, Ill.: Rand McNally, 1976.

Thorndike, R. L. *Personnel Selection*. New York: John Wiley, 1949.

Training and Development

Clark, K. E., and M. B. Clark. *Measures of Leadership*. West Orange, N.J.: Leadership Library of America, 1990.

Craig, R. L. *Training and Development Handbook*, 2d ed. New York: McGraw-Hill, 1976.

Hinrichs, J. H. "Personnel Training." In M. D. Dunnette, ed., *Handbook of Industrial and Organizational Psychology*. Skokie, Ill.: Rand McNally, 1976.

Kirkpatrick, D. L. "Evaluation of Training." In R. L. Craig, ed., *Training and Development Handbook*, 2d ed. New York: McGraw-Hill, 1976.

Sorcher, M. "Behavior Modeling and Motivational Skills." In J. R. Hackman, E. E. Lawler, and L. W. Porter, eds., *Perspectives on Behavior in Organizations*, 2d. ed. New York: McGraw-Hill, 1983.

Employee Motivation and Management

Herzberg, F. *Work and the Nature of Man*. Cleveland: World, 1966.

Herzberg, F., B. Mausner, and B. B. Snyderman. *The Motivation of Work*. New York: Wiley, 1959.

Kelley, R. E. *The Gold Collar Worker*. Reading, Mass.: Addison-Wesley, 1985.

Latham, G. P., and K. N. Wexley. *Increasing Productivity Through Performance Appraisal*. Reading, Mass.: Addison-Wesley, 1981.

Lawler, E. E. *Pay and Organizational Effectiveness: A Psychological View*. New York: McGraw-Hill, 1971.

Likert, R. *New Patterns of Management*. New York: McGraw-Hill, 1961.

Locke, E. A. "The Nature and Causes of Job Satisfaction." In M. D. Dunnette, ed., *Handbook of Industrial and Organizational Psychology*. Skokie, Ill.: Rand McNally, 1976.

Maslow, A. H. *Motivation and Personality*, 2d ed. New York: Harper and Row, 1970.

McClelland, D. C. *The Achieving Society*. New York: Free Press, 1961.

Mobley, W. H. *Employee Turnover: Causes, Consequences, and Control*. Reading, Mass.: Addison-Wesley, 1982.

Porter, L. W., and E. E. Lawler. *Managerial Attitudes and Performance*. Homewood, Ill.: Irwin, 1968.

Ronen, S. *Flexible Working Hours: An Innovation in the Quality of Working Life*. New York: McGraw-Hill, 1981.

Steers, R. M., and L. W. Porter, eds. *Motivation and Work Behavior*. New York: McGraw-Hill, 1975.

Stodgill, R. M. *Handbook of Leadership: A Survey of Theory and Research*. New York: Free Press, 1974.

Vroom, V. H. *Work and Motivation*. New York: Wiley, 1964.

Vroom, V. H., and P. W. Yetton. *Leadership and Decision-Making*. Pittsburgh: University of Pittsburgh Press, 1973.

Financial Aspects of Employment Strategies

Mercer, M. M. "Turnover: Reducing the Costs." *Personnel* 65 (1988): 36–42.

Phillips, J. J. *The Development of a Human Resources Effectiveness Index*. Ph.D. diss., University of Alabama, 1988. Available from Ann Arbor, Mich.: University Microfilms International, 1988.

Phillips, J. J. *Evaluating the Human Resources Function*. San Francisco: Jossey-Bass, 1990.

Swanson, R. A., and D. B. Gradous. *Forecasting the Financial Benefits of Human Resource Development*. San Francisco: Jossey-Bass, 1988.

Job Design

Chapanis, A. "Engineering Psychology." In M. D. Dunnette, ed., *Handbook of Industrial and Organizational Psychology*. Skokie, Ill.: Rand McNally, 1976.

Fiedler, F. E. "Engineer the Job to Fit the Manager." *Harvard Business Review*, 43 (1965), 115–122.

Hackman, J. R., E. E. Lawler, and L. W. Porter, eds., *Perspectives on Behavior in Organizations*. New York: McGraw-Hill, 1977.

Hackman, J. R., and G. R. Oldham. *Work Redesign*. Reading, Mass.: Addison-Wesley, 1980.

McCormick, E. J., and M. S. Sanders. *Human Factors in Engineering and Design*. New York: McGraw-Hill, 1982.

Labor Force

1988 ASPA Labor Shortage Survey. Alexandria, Va.: Society for Human Resource Management, 1988.

Greller, M. *From Baby Boom to Baby Bust*. Reading, Mass.: Addison-Wesley, 1989.

Marketing

Reis, A., and J. Trout. *Positioning: The Battle for Your Mind*. New York: McGraw-Hill, 1981.

Alternative Staffing Approaches

Nollen, S. D., and V. H. Martin. *Alternative Work Schedules, Part I: Flextime*. New York: AMACOM, 1978.

Nye, D. *Alternative Staffing Strategies*. Washington, D.C.: Bureau of National Affairs, 1988.

Employment: General Interest

Muchinsky, P. M. *"Psychology Applied to Work*, 2d ed. Chicago: Dorsey, 1987.

Schultz, D. P., and S. E. Schultz. *Psychology and Industry Today* 4th ed. New York: Macmillan, 1986.

Taylor, F. W. *The Principles of Scientific Management.* New York: Harper, 1911.

Scott, W. D. *Increasing Human Efficiency in Business.* New York: Macmillan, 1911.

Mankin, D., R. E. Ames, Jr., and M. A. Grodsky, eds. *Classics of Industrial and Organizational Psychology.* Oak Park, Ill.: Moore Publishing Co., 1980.

March, J. G. *Handbook of Organizations.* Skokie, Ill.: Rand McNally, 1965.

Index

Age Discrimination Act of 1978, 216–217
American Society of Personnel Administrators (ASPA), xviii, 11
Arizona State University, 36, 139
Assessment centers, 99–100
Associated Spring, 65
Association of National Advertisers, 18
AT&T, xvi

Baby boom/baby bust, xvii
Barnes Group, Inc., 65
Bona-fide occupational requirements (BFOQs), 211–215, 220
Buyer's remorse, 115

Candidate's vision of employment, the: candidate research, role of, 64–69; importance of, 59; total employment purchase, the, 60–64
Carrier International, 3
Challenges, presenting, 128–130
Chapman, Bob, 65
Chrysler Corporation, 48
Civil Rights Act of 1964, Title VII of, 215, 218–219
Clairol hair-dye campaign, 59, 68, 82
Compensation, xviii; competitive employer strategies, 146–148; fair, 130–132; mistakes in, 31, 38; motivation and, 130–132
Competitive employer, the: alternative staffing strategies, 149–151; compensation strategies, 146–148; geography, creative use of, 152–153; importance of, 145, 154; technological advances, 151–152; training strategies, 148–149

Competive Equation self-test: description of, 155–156; how to use, 156–158; questionnaire for, 159–209
Consolidated Omnibus Budget Reconciliation Act (COBRA), 219
Credibility, management, 3
CUC International, 121
Customer service, at Wells Fargo Bank, 50
Customer-supplier partnership management model, xx–xxi

D'Ambrosio, Jeannie, 121
Definite, being: defining the kind of employee you need, 41–43; job analysis, 44–57, 104–106
Denne, Patricia, 43
Design, job, 129
Diamond Star Motors, 48, 94
Diversity in the workforce, xvii

Eder, Peter, 18
Employment Eligibility Verification Form, 217
Employment Retirement Income Security Act of 1974 (ERISA), 219
Engineer shortage, 66
Enlargement, job, 130
Enrichment, job, 130
Environmental requirements, 46–47, 53–55, 105–106
Equal Employment Opportunity Commission (EEOC), 215
Equal Employment Opportunity (EEO) laws and regulations: do's and don'ts regarding, 222–223; employee safety and health

Equal Employment Opportunity (EEO)
  (continued)
  regulations, 217–218; employment
  regulations, 215–217; introduction
  to, 213–215; labor union
  regulations, 219; pay and benefits
  regulations, 218–219; questions and
  answers regarding, 220–222
Equal Pay Act of 1963, 218
Executive Order 11246, 215
Executive Order 11701, 216
Executive Order 19914, 216

Fair Labor Standards Act of 1938, as
  amended, 218
Family responsibilities, xvi
Fasolo, John, 65
Festinger, Leon, 115
Focus groups, 64
*Forecasting the Financial Benefits of
  Human Resource Development*
  (Swanson and Gradous), 12

Gandhi, Mohandas K., 127
General Aptitude Test Battery (GATB),
  48
Genghis Khan, 127
Geography, creative use of, 152–153
Gould, Robert, 41–42
Gradous, Deane, 12

Hackman, J. Richard, 130
Henry, Sarah, 48
Herzberg, Frederick, 130–132
Hickel, Maggie, 66
Hitler, Adolf, 127
Hours, working longer, xviii
Housing, employer-provided, 153
Human resources effectiveness index, 11

Iacocca, Lee, 127
IBM, xvi
Ideal job, desire for, 68
Illinois Department of Employment
  Security, 48
Immigration Reform and Control Act
  of 1986, 217
Industry and professional associations,
  candidate research and, 67
Interviewing: importance of, 101–102;

job analysis and, 104–106; mistakes
  in, 30–31, 38; as a screening
  method, 102–103

Job analysis: customer service at Wells
  Fargo Bank, 50; description of, 44;
  environmental requirements, 46–47,
  53–55, 105–106; how to use,
  49–50, 57; interviewing and,
  104–106; motivational requirements, 46, 52–53, 105; performance
  requirements, 44–45, 51, 104;
  screening and selection process at
  Diamond Star Motors, 48, 94;
  summary form, 56

Kennedy, John F., 127
King, Martin Luther, Jr., 127
Kishbaugh, Lyle, 3

Labor-Management Relations Act
  (Taft-Hartley Act of 1947), 219
Laws. *See* Equal Employment
  Opportunity laws and regulations
Leadership: effectiveness of, 125–127;
  mistakes in, 33–34, 38
Lincoln, Abraham, 127
Lubner, Charles, 68

Management: credibility of, 3;
  customer-supplier partnership
  model of, xx–xxi; effectiveness of,
  125–126; master-slave model of, xv,
  xx; mistakes in, 33–34, 38; parent-
  child model of, xv–xviii, xxi
Manufacturing recruiting, at Barnes
  Group, 65
Market-driven recruiting:
  communicating with the target,
  79–82; competition in, 82–89; how
  to use, 89–91; importance of,
  71–73; reaching the target
  candidates, 77–79; for shift work,
  90; sizing the target market, 73–77;
  at Waldenbooks, 81
Marketing in an employment context:
  employment as a buying process,
  5–9; importance of, 1–5; removing
  reasons to say no to change, 13–19;
  resistances to, 9–12

Master-slave management model, xv, xxi
Meaningful work, 128–129
Mercer, Michael, 132–133
Mitsubishi, 48
Morale, mistakes in, 34–36, 39
Motivation: compensation and, 130–132; factors, 82; requirements, 46, 52–53, 105

National Labor Relations Act of 1935 (Wagner Act), 219
National Labor Relations Board (NLRB), 219
New employees. *See* Orientation; Training
New England Spring Manufacturers Association, 65
Noncompetitive employment practices: Joe Warmbody example, 21–26; what went wrong at Wonderful Widgets, 26–39
Nontraditional employment contracts, 151
Nontraditional populations, as a source of employees, 151

Objections, handling, 109–112
Occupational Safety and Health Act of 1970, 217
Occupational Safety and Health Administration (OSHA), 217
Orientation: company-centered, 117, 118; employee-centered, 117–120; importance of, 115–116; mistakes in, 31–32, 38, 120

Palmer, Susan, 50
Parent-child management model, xv–xviii, xx–xxi
Patton, George, 127
Pepperidge Farm, 43
Performance requirements, 44–45, 51, 104
Phillips, Jack J., 11
Planning, mistakes in, 27
Positioning: The Battle for Your Mind (Trout and Ries), 86
Pregnancy Discrimination Act of 1978, 216

Privacy Act of 1974, 216
Professional and industry associations, candidate research and, 67
Psychological tests, 96–97, 99

Reagan, Ronald, 127
Recruiters, candidate research and professional, 67–69
Recruiting: manufacturing, 65; market-driven, 71–91; mistakes in, 28–29, 38; for shift work, 90
Regulations. *See* Equal Employment Opportunity laws and regulations
Research, candidate: engineer shortage, 66; focus groups, 64; ideal job, desire for, 68; industry and professional associations, 67; manufacturing recruiting at Barnes Group, 65; professional recruiters, 67–69; turnover surveys, 66–67
Retention-oriented, being: importance of, 123; managing for retention, 123–132. *See also* Turnover
Ries, Al, 86
Roosevelt, Franklin D., 127

Saratoga Institute, 11
Satellite offices, 153
Satisfaction, surveys measuring employee, 139–142
Scalia, Frank, 65
Screening and selection process: assessment centers, 99–100; at Diamond Star Motors, 48, 94; self-screening, 94–95; simulations, 100–101; testing, 95–99; trial periods, 95
Secor Bank, 11
Selective sales approach to hiring: importance of, 93; interviewing, 101–106; objections, handling, 109–112; realistic expectations in, 108–112; sales skill, role of, 106–107; screening and selecting, 94–101
Self-screening, 94–95
Shannon, Maureen, 81
Shegirian, Roseanne, 69
Shift work, recruiting for, 90
Shipper, Frank, 36, 139–140

Simulations, 100–101
Skills: shortages, xvii, 10; tests, 96;
    tiered skills arrangements, 149–150
Small Business Administration (SBA),
    xviii
Society for Human Resources
    Management, xviii, 11
Society of Women Engineers, 66
State workers' compensation laws,
    217–218
Substance abuse problems, xvi
Surveys: employee satisfaction,
    139–142; turnover, 66–67
Swanson, Richard, 12

Taft-Hartley Act of 1947 (Labor-
    Management Relations Act), 219
Technological advances, 151–152
Telecommuting, 153
Testing: good tests versus bad tests,
    98–99; pros and cons of, 95–96;
    psychological tests, 96–97, 99; skill
    tests, 96
Tiered skills arrangements, 149–150
Title VII of the Civil Rights Act of
    1964, 215, 218–219
Towers-Perrin, 48
Training: competitive employer
    strategies, 148–149; at CUC
    International, 121; importance of,
    120–122; mistakes in, 32, 38
Transportation: difficulties with, xvi;

employer-provided, 153
Trial periods, 95
Trout, Jack, 86
*Turning Your Human Resource
    Department into a Profit Center*
    (Mercer), 132–133
Turnover: damage caused by, 132–133;
    do you really have a problem?, 134;
    mistakes in, 36–37, 39; positive
    action to prevent, 137–138; surveys
    regarding, 66–67; who's
    vulnerable?, 135–137; why do
    valuable employees leave?, 135. *See
    also* Retention-oriented, being

University of Minnesota, Training and
    Development Research Center of, 12

Vietnam Era Veterans' Readjustment
    Act of 1974, 216
Vocational Rehabilitation Act of 1973,
    216

Wages. *See* Compensation
Wagner Act (National Labor Relations
    Act of 1935), 219
Waldenbooks, 81
Wells Fargo Bank, 50
Wilson, Clark, 33, 36, 127
Windsor Manufacturing, 65
Workers' compensation laws, state,
    217–218

About the Authors

Kathleen Groll Connolly writes on a variety of business topics, in addition to being a seminar instructor and consultant on marketing. She is the founding editor of a marketing newsletter, *The Business Partner*. She was a marketing director in the computer industry prior to launching her own business in 1988. A native of Pittsburgh, she holds a B.A. in writing from the Pennsylvania State University and an M.B.A. in marketing from New York University.

Paul M. Connolly, Ph.D., has done extensive work in leadership development, management development, employee morale, turnover, survey and test design, and validation for employment purposes. He is currently authoring a survey to help managers work more successfully with new staff members. He recently co-authored *The Survey of Organization Values* with psychologist Clark Wilson. He is a licensed industrial/organizational psychologist and has consulted with more than 150 firms over the past thirteen years. A native of Natick, Massachusetts, Connolly is a graduate of Holy Cross College and earned his Ph.D. at Fordham University.

The Connollys operate Performance Programs, a human resources consulting firm, in Norwalk, Connecticut. They have been married for five years and have one son, Jason.

Presentation

Who's purchased a major item recently / House / Car / Owner in self
question
— write down purchase process. Pg 6.

Books Philips Jack - Eval HR fx. Jossey-Bass

Dev Pts -

Always recognize that ee's could be attracted to others.
- What would attract you to another oppty at = $$.
- Exit intrs.

Ref Questions: p34 Table 2. 2/3 on mgmt/leadership effectiveness
For new ee: develop motivational profile / criteria.

Bill Terry   617.699.6113   Russia Core Equipmt.

EB ?   E.S.
- how measure
- e'ee metrics ?

Saville
Cask Smith
Barry Shaffer

*
TK-little - be overlooked or rejected due
to 15 yrs in own business. +
away from HR Generalist Roles.